Legal Solutions
in Electronic Reserves
and the Electronic Delivery
of Interlibrary Loan

Legal Solutions in Electronic Reserves and the Electronic Delivery of Interlibrary Loan has been co-published simultaneously as *Journal of Interlibrary Loan, Document Delivery & Information Supply*, Volume 14, Number 3 2004.

The *Journal of Interlibrary Loan, Document Delivery & Information Supply*™ Monographic "Separates"

(formerly the *Journal of Interlibrary Loan & Information Supply*)*

For information on previous issues of the *Journal of Interlibrary Loan & Information Supply* series, edited by Leslie R. Morris, please contact: The Haworth Press, Inc., 10 Alice Street, Binghamton, NY 13904-1580 USA.

Below is a list of "separates," which in serials librarianship means a special issue simultaneously published as a journal issue or double-issue *and* as a "separate" hardbound monograph. (This is a format which we also call a "DocuSerial.")

"Separates" are published because specialized libraries or professionals may wish to purchase a specific thematic issue by itself in a format which can be separately cataloged and shelved, as opposed to purchasing the journal on an on-going basis. Faculty members may also more easily consider a "separate" for classroom adoption.

"Separates" are carefully classified separately with the major book jobbers so that the journal tie-in can be noted on new book order slips to avoid duplicate purchasing.

You may wish to visit Haworth's Website at . . .

http://www.HaworthPress.com

. . . to search our online catalog for complete tables of contents of these separates and related publications.

You may also call 1-800-HAWORTH (outside US/Canada: 607-722-5857), or Fax 1-800-895-0582 (outside US/Canada: 607-771-0012), or e-mail at:

docdelivery@haworthpress.com

Legal Solutions in Electronic Reserves and the Electronic Delivery of Interlibrary Loan, by Janet Brennan Croft (Vol. 14, No. 3, 2004). *Guides librarians through the process of developing legal policies for their electronic resources to protect patrons' rights and to avoid copyright infringement.*

Electronic Reserve: A Manual and Guide for Library Staff Members, by Lori Driscoll (Vol. 14, No. 1, 2003). *A comprehensive guide to establishing and maintaining effective electronic reserve services.*

Interlibrary Loan and Document Delivery in the Larger Academic Library: A Guide for University, Research, and Larger Public Libraries, by Lee Andrew Hilyer (Vol. 13, No. 1/2, 2002). *A concise but thorough introductory guide to the daily operation of an interlibrary loan department.*

Ariel: Internet Transmission Software for Document Delivery, edited by Gary Ives (Vol. 10, No. 4, 2000). *"Useful . . . Instructive. Answers are provided to questions continually asked by other Ariel users as well as potential users." (Marilyn C. Grush, MLS, Coordinator, Interlibrary Loan/Document Delivery, University of Delaware)*

Information Delivery in the 21st Century: Proceedings of the Fourth International Conference on Fee-Based Information Services in Libraries, edited by Suzanne M. Ward, Yem S. Fong, and Tammy Nickelson Dearie (Vol. 10, No. 1, 1999). *"This book is an excellent overview of the issues and realities of fee-based information services in academic and public libraries. . . . It is especially insightful for public libraries considering fee-based services. . . . An excellent addition to any library's collection." (Kathy Gillespie Tomajko, MLn, BS, Department Head, Reference Services, Georgia Institute of Technology Library and Information Center)*

The Economics of Access versus Ownership: The Costs and Benefits of Access to Scholarly Articles via Interlibrary Loan and Journal Subscriptions, by Bruce R. Kingma, PhD (Vol. 6, No. 3, 1996). *"Presents a well-constructed and well-described study and a consequent set of conclusions about the cooperative economics of borrowing versus owning library journal subscriptions. . . A well-done and much needed book." (Catholic Library World)*

Information Brokers: Case Studies of Successful Ventures, by Alice Jane Holland Johnson, MLS (Vol. 5, No. 2, 1995). *"The insights in this compilation give practical overviews that are applicable to information professionals interested in becoming information brokers, starting their own brokerages, or adding this function to their existing library service." (Journal of Interlibrary Loan, Document Delivery & Information Supply)*

Interlibrary Loan of Alternative Format Materials: A Balanced Sourcebook,* edited by Bruce S. Massis, MLS, MA and Winnie Vitzansky (Vol. 3, No. 1/2, 1993). *"Essential for interlibrary loan departments serving blind or visually handicapped patrons. . . . An enlightening survey of the state of the art in international lending of nonprint library materials." (Information Technology and Libraries)*

Legal Solutions in Electronic Reserves and the Electronic Delivery of Interlibrary Loan

Janet Brennan Croft

Legal Solutions in Electronic Reserves and the Electronic Delivery of Interlibrary Loan has been co-published simultaneously as *Journal of Interlibrary Loan, Document Delivery & Information Supply*, Volume 14, Number 3 2004.

The Haworth Information Press®
An Imprint of The Haworth Press, Inc.

New York • London • Victoria (AU)
www.HaworthPress.com

Published by

The Haworth Information Press®, 10 Alice Street, Binghamton, NY 13904-1580 USA

The Haworth Information Press® is an imprint of The Haworth Press, Inc., 10 Alice Street, Binghamton, NY 13904-1580 USA.

Legal Solutions in Electronic Reserves and the Electronic Delivery of Interlibrary Loan has been co-published simultaneously as *Journal of Interlibrary Loan, Document Delivery & Information Supply*™, Volume 14, Number 3 2004.

Cover design by Marylouise E. Doyle.

Cover photo credit: Stacie L. Graves.

Library of Congress Cataloging-in-Publication Data

Croft, Janet Brennan.
    Legal solutions in electronic reserves and the electronic delivery of interlibrary loan / Janet Brennan Croft.
        p. cm.
    "Co-published simultaneously as Journal of interlibrary loan, document delivery & information supply, volume 14, number 3, 2004."
    Includes bibliographical references and index.
    ISBN 0-7890-2558-2 (alk. paper) – ISBN 0-7890-2559-0 (pbk. : alk. paper)
    1. Interlibrary loans–Law and legislation–United States. 2. Electronic reserve collections in libraries–Law and legislation–United States. 3. Fair use (Copyright)–United States. I. Journal of interlibrary loan, document delivery & information supply. II. Title.
KF4315.C76 2004
346.7304'82–dc22
                                      2003027727

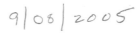

Indexing, Abstracting & Website/Internet Coverage

Journal of Interlibrary Loan, Document Delivery & Information Supply

This section provides you with a list of major indexing & abstracting services. That is to say, each service began covering this periodical during the year noted in the right column. Most Websites which are listed below have indicated that they will either post, disseminate, compile, archive, cite or alert their own Website users with research-based content from this work. (This list is as current as the copyright date of this publication.)

(continued)

(continued)

*Special Bibliographic Notes related to special journal issues
(separates) and indexing/abstracting:*

- indexing/abstracting services in this list will also cover material in any "separate" that is co-published simultaneously with Haworth's special thematic journal issue or DocuSerial. Indexing/abstracting usually covers material at the article/chapter level.
- monographic co-editions are intended for either non-subscribers or libraries which intend to purchase a second copy for their circulating collections.
- monographic co-editions are reported to all jobbers/wholesalers/approval plans. The source journal is listed as the "series" to assist the prevention of duplicate purchasing in the same manner utilized for books-in-series.
- to facilitate user/access services all indexing/abstracting services are encouraged to utilize the co-indexing entry note indicated at the bottom of the first page of each article/chapter/contribution.
- this is intended to assist a library user of any reference tool (whether print, electronic, online, or CD-ROM) to locate the monographic version if the library has purchased this version but not a subscription to the source journal.
- individual articles/chapters in any Haworth publication are also available through the Haworth Document Delivery Service (HDDS).

Legal Solutions in Electronic Reserves and the Electronic Delivery of Interlibrary Loan

CONTENTS

Disclaimer

The information presented in this volume is not intended to replace the advice of legal counsel. The author is not a lawyer or legal professional, and strongly recommends that readers approach their institution's counsel with any questions or doubts about their particular situation.

ABOUT THE AUTHOR

Janet Brennan Croft, MLS, is Head of Access Services at the University of Oklahoma Libraries. She earned her MLS at Indiana University in 1983. She has written on library issues for *College & Undergraduate Libraries*, *Interlending and Document Supply* (her 2002 article on interlibrary loan and model licenses was named outstanding paper of the year), *Journal of Access Services*, and *Journal of Academic Libraries* (forthcoming). She is active in the Popular Culture Association, the Southwest/Texas Popular Culture Association, and the Mythopoeic Society.

Ms. Croft is also the author of *War and the Works of J.R.R. Tolkien* (Greenwood Press, 2004) and the editor of *Tolkien on Film: Essays of Peter Jackson's The Lord of the Rings* (Mythopoeic Press, 2004).

Acknowledgments

The author wishes to thank Molly Murphy, Document Delivery Librarian at the University of Oklahoma, for her advice on the Interlibrary Loan chapter. She also thanks her husband, Duane Croft, for his assistance in locating relevant cases.

Introduction

Libraries exist in an increasingly complex and rapidly changing technological and legal landscape. The most important legal issue for both electronic reserves and electronic delivery of interlibrary loan is, of course, copyright compliance. Staying within the law, while facilitating fair use of information for our patrons, is becoming a more complicated process every year. Technology and the law play leapfrog as innovations create a need for new regulations and new regulations breed innovations designed to bypass them. The balance of power seesaws between the interests of consumers seeking information and entertainment and those of businesses seeking profit.

Libraries have long been places where the needs of consumers are preferred as far as legally allowed, while the rights of copyright holders are respected but not extended beyond their legal limits. As Laura Gasaway points out:

> Most librarians are law-abiding citizens who want to comply with the copyright law. Unrealistic restrictions, outright denial of use . . . and unreasonable royalty fees on the part of publishers may discourage compliance. (Gasaway "Copyright Considerations" 131)

The core mission of libraries is to provide access to information, as much as possible without direct charge, for their user group. Libraries seek to minimize expense to the consumer by spreading the cost of the product across their entire income base of potential users (taxpayers or students, for example). In the United States, we are fortunate that the doctrine of "first sale" allows us to lend the material we own to our users without any addi-

[Haworth co-indexing entry note]: "Introduction." Croft, Janet Brennan. Co-published simultaneously in *Journal of Interlibrary Loan, Document Delivery & Information Supply* (The Haworth Information Press, an imprint of The Haworth Press, Inc.) Vol. 14, No. 3, 2004, pp. 1-3; and: *Legal Solutions in Electronic Reserves and the Electronic Delivery of Interlibrary Loan* (Janet Brennan Croft) The Haworth Information Press, an imprint of The Haworth Press, Inc., 2004, pp. 1-3. Single or multiple copies of this article are available for a fee from The Haworth Document Delivery Service [1-800-HAWORTH, 9:00 a.m. - 5:00 p.m. (EST). E-mail address: docdelivery@haworthpress.com].

http://www.haworthpress.com/web/JILIS
Digital Object Identifier: 10.1300/J110v14n03_01

tional remuneration to its author. The "first sale" rule is "the concept that copyright holders only control the first sale of their works, after which purchasers may give them away, sell them, or otherwise pass them along" (Heins "Introduction" 4). "First sale" made it easy to deal with copyright issues when information existed only in tangible physical forms owned outright by the library, but photocopying and digitization technologies have complicated the situation. As Duane Webster has pointed out:

> Previously, as owner of a particular copy of a book, a library was entitled to set the terms of patron access to that copy. In the new world of libraries as licensee of a digital work subject to technological measures, the library may be denied such right. (Webster 3)

Information producers, in contrast to libraries, seek to maximize profit, and one way to do this is to charge for every possible access to their product. New forms of technology, collectively known as Digital Rights Management, are providing information producers with new ways to organize, protect, supply and control access to and use of their information. Additionally, more producers are offering their products only on a contractual basis, where they can set terms that may negate the fair use exceptions that consumers are accustomed to view as their rights under copyright law. Under these contracts, the library does not actually own the material, but only pays for access to it, and producers may argue that "first sale" and other fair use exceptions do not apply. Unfortunately, the current legal climate seems to favor business over the consumer and libraries are caught in the middle, but there are signs (particularly the abandonment of attempts to draft an acceptable version of the Uniform Computer Information Transactions Act (UCITA) by the National Conference of Commissioners on Uniform State Laws) that the situation may be changing.

Another legal issue that affects electronic reserves and interlibrary loan is patron confidentiality. We feel a professional responsibility (and in most cases are required by state law) to protect our patrons from unwarranted intrusion into their private reading and research. Nevertheless, we must also be prepared to respect legitimate requests for information on a patron's library activities under a properly justified subpoena or search warrant. The chilling effects of USA PATRIOT Act on patron confidentiality understandably disturb librarians. A subpoena or search warrant can be obtained on a far lower level of suspicion than probable cause, and the gag order clause included in the Act prevents us from discussing anything we might consider an abuse of the Act. However, we must also consider less obvious and controversial confidentiality issues such as instructor's desire to know if students have read their assignments, or copyright compliance requirements for retaining interlibrary loan records.

This volume will also consider current and pending legislation that might affect electronic reserves and interlibrary loan. The similarities and differences between traditional and electronic reserves and interlibrary loan will be analyzed for their legal implications, and the recommended components of policies and procedures listed and discussed. The author is not a lawyer and recommends that you seek the advice of your institution's counsel when in doubt concerning your particular situation.

Janet Brennan Croft

Chapter 1

Copyright Basics

1. WHAT LAWS COVER COPYRIGHT FOR LIBRARIANS AND EDUCATORS?

- The *Copyright Act of 1976*, especially sections 107 (Fair Use), 108 (Reproduction by Libraries and Archives), 109 (Effect of Transfer of Particular Copy or Phonorecord) and 110 (Exemption of Certain Performances and Displays), is the main body of applicable law.
- *Amendments* to the 1976 act cover software, audio/visual materials and international copyright.
- The *Digital Millennium Copyright Act* (DMCA) of 1998 prohibits circumvention of technological measures designed to control access to copyrighted material and allows manufacturers to impose technological controls on their works that are more restrictive than preceding laws allow.
- The *Term Extension Act* ("Sonny Bono Act") of 1998 adds twenty years to the duration of copyrights.
- The *Technology, Education and Copyright Harmonization* (TEACH) Act of 2002 permits specified uses of digitized materials in distance education, provided the institution complies with certain stringent requirements.

All of these can be found online at http://www.copyright.gov/laws/. Sections 107, 108, 109 and 110 are reproduced in Appendix 1 of this paper. There are also several sets of widely used guidelines, as follows.

[Haworth co-indexing entry note]: "Copyright Basics." Croft, Janet Brennan. Co-published simultaneously in *Journal of Interlibrary Loan, Document Delivery & Information Supply* (The Haworth Information Press, an imprint of The Haworth Press, Inc.) Vol. 14, No. 3, 2004, pp. 5-15; and: *Legal Solutions in Electronic Reserves and the Electronic Delivery of Interlibrary Loan* (Janet Brennan Croft) The Haworth Information Press, an imprint of The Haworth Press, Inc., 2004, pp. 5-15. Single or multiple copies of this article are available for a fee from The Haworth Document Delivery Service [1-800-HAWORTH, 9:00 a.m. - 5:00 p.m. (EST). E-mail address: docdelivery@haworthpress.com].

http://www.haworthpress.com/web/JILIS
Digital Object Identifier: 10.1300/J110v14n03_02

2. SECURING COPYRIGHT:
WHAT IS PROTECTED BY COPYRIGHT?

"Copyright" secures certain rights to someone who creates a work that is "fixed in a tangible form of expression," as described in the Copyright Act of 1976. *Copyright exists automatically* from the moment the item is created; it is not necessary to formally publish or register a work for it to be copyrighted. The following types of works are included and specific definitions for each form can be found at the Website previously listed:

- Literary works
- Musical works, including any accompanying words
- Dramatic works, including any accompanying music
- Pantomimes and choreographic works
- Pictorial, graphic and sculptural works
- Motion pictures and other audiovisual works
- Sound recordings
- Architectural works.

A work that is not *"fixed"* is not protected; this might include such works as improvised speeches or songs that have neither been written out in advance, nor recorded during performance. An unpublished letter or diary is "fixed" and therefore copyrighted. Ideas cannot be copyrighted until fixed in a tangible form. And "works consisting *entirely* of information that is common property and containing no original authorship" cannot be copyrighted–this includes items like calendars, tables of weights and measures, etc. (*Copyright Basics* 4-5).

3. RIGHTS OF THE COPYRIGHT HOLDER

The copyright holder has certain rights:

- To *reproduce* the work
- To *prepare derivative works* based upon the work
- To *distribute* the work
- To *perform* the work publicly
- To *display* the work publicly.

These rights may be signed over piecemeal to other parties; for example, the author of a book may sell the film rights to one company and the book-on-tape rights to another. These rights are limited by first sale doctrine (section 109(a)), which allows someone who buys a book or other copyrighted item to resell, give away, rent, or lend it to someone else; this is the exception that allows libraries to operate.[1] The author's rights are also limited by fair use exceptions.

4. EXPIRATION OF COPYRIGHT

How long does a work stay under copyright? It depends on several factors: when the work was first fixed in a tangible form or published, whether the author is alive or dead, and whether it is a work for hire, a group work, or an anonymous work.

The importance of limiting the time a work remains under copyright was understood by the framers of the Constitution, who wrote in Article 1, Section 8, that Congress has the power "[t]o promote the Progress of Science and useful Arts, by securing for limited Times to Authors and Inventors the exclusive Right to their respective Writings and Discoveries." The *exclusive rights* encourage creators to produce work because they alone will profit from it for a certain amount of time, the idea being that "creative people need the promise of financial reward to motivate them to produce art, music, literature and scientific innovation" (Heins "Introduction" 1). The balancing *limitation on time* allows works to eventually pass into the public domain, where they can be used as a basis for further works by anybody who wishes to do so. If a work is in the public domain, anyone can "publish, sell, adapt, translate, record, or perform" it without having to pay permission fees (Heins "Introduction" 5). Duane Webster points out that the "Sonny Bono Act" and other copyright term extension initiatives threaten the public domain and have

> [a] profound and negative effect on librarians and other scholars by prohibiting the republication and dissemination of older works that have no commercial value, yet are of strong interest to the scholarly community. (Webster 6)

In simplified form:

- If the work was created *after January 1, 1978*: Copyright is for the author's life plus 70 years. For group works, copyright expires 70 years after the last surviving author's death. If an item is a "work for hire" (some educational or corporate works) or anonymous, copyright lasts 95 years from publication or 120 years from creation, whichever comes first.

- If the work was created *before January 1, 1978*: Copyright lasts a maximum of 95 years from date of publication, depending on circumstances (such as whether its copyright was renewed or not). A work created in 1977 will not enter the public domain until 2072.
- If the work was created *before 1923*: It is in the public domain, that is, the work is not copyrighted and may be used freely.
- *Federal government publications* are not copyrighted under section 105.
- There are some *limited exemptions* for libraries from the Term Extension Act; in the last 20 years of a work's term, a library or archive may be able to reproduce and distribute a work if certain conditions are met.

Laura Gasaway's detailed chart on determining whether a work is likely to be under copyright is available at http://www.unc.edu/~unclng/public-d. htm. If in doubt, check the work through one of the sources of permission listed in Appendix 3, or the additional sources provided by Georgia Harper at http://www.utsystem.edu/ogc/intellectualproperty/permissn.htm. The U.S. Copyright Office provides a guide to researching the copyright status of a work at http://www.copyright.gov/circs/circ22.html.

Interestingly, the concept of creative work as intellectual "property" is recent, dating back only to the mid-1960s. As Marjorie Heins points out, "Viewing creativity as property, 'intellectual' or otherwise, leads to the presumption that it can and should be owned and controlled forever" (Heins "Introduction" 2). But creativity is an inexhaustible resource and a creative product like a book is not used up if read over and over again; therefore, one could conclude that "works of the imagination do not need a system of control to assure that they are not depleted; they only need a system that encourages their creation and fairly rewards their creators" (Heins "Introduction" 2). Some people advocate a loosening of copyright laws in the cyber era on this basis, ranging from radical groups preaching "property is theft," to respected copyright attorneys proposing viable alternate systems to established copyright law, to organizations attempting to create new models for scholarly publishing.

5. FAIR USE

The concept of "Fair Use" provides educators, librarians, researchers and other individuals with limited ways to use copyrighted material without violating the rights of the author. Fair Use is covered under section

107 of the Copyright Law and allows the public to "share, enjoy, criticize, parody, and build on the works of others" (Heins "Executive Summary" 2). Fair Use is a defense against charges of infringement, although some also see it as a right (Gasaway "Copyright Considerations" 132, note 17). To determine if an intended use is fair, the user must take into consideration the following *four factors*:

- The *purpose and character of the use*, including whether such use is of a commercial nature or is for nonprofit educational purposes. A non-profit institution is granted greater leeway in using copyrighted material than a for-profit company.
- The *nature of the copyrighted work*. Is the original work creative or factual? Using a factual work is more likely to be permitted than using a creative work. Is it a "consumable" item, like a workbook? Copying a consumable item is rarely fair use.
- The *amount and substantiality of the portion used* in relation to the copyrighted work as a whole. Using the whole work or a major portion of it is not fair use and neither is using only the "heart of the work."
- The *effect of the use upon the potential market* for or value of the copyrighted work. Will it affect sales adversely?

The complex interplay of these factors must be judged on a *case-by-case* basis; there are no hard and fast rules for the user. A useful checklist has been developed by Kenneth Crews: http://www.copyright.iupui.edu/fairuse.htm. All factors must be considered; the fact that the copying is being done by a non-profit institution does not automatically make all uses permissible.

6. SPECIAL ALLOWANCES FOR LIBRARY COPYING, RESERVES, INTERLIBRARY LOAN AND TEACHING

Additionally, libraries also have the right under Section 108 to make copies of a work for individual users, interlibrary loan, or preservation, if certain conditions are met:

- The library must be *open to the public or researchers* from outside the institution
- The copies must be made *without a profit* to the library

- Copies must *include a standard notice* of responsibility for copyright violations
- There can be *no "systematic" copying* of works (for example, a library cannot systematically photocopy articles from the new issue of a journal each month to send to a routing list of instructors).

When making copies for individuals:

- The copy must become the *property of the user*
- To the best of the library's knowledge, the user must plan to use it only for *private research or study*
- The library must *display the official warning* about responsibility for copyright violations where orders for copies are taken
- In order to copy an entire work, such as a whole book, the library must determine that it *cannot buy a copy at a fair price.*

For interlibrary loan, both libraries must meet all of these requirements, plus additional CONTU guidelines, to be discussed.

When making copies for preservation:

- The library must be replacing a work that is damaged, lost, stolen, or in an obsolete format
- The library must determine that a replacement (or the obsolete equipment needed to display or perform an audio-visual item) cannot be purchased at a fair price
- The replacement can be used only in the library
- Only three copies can be made.

Section 110 provides exemptions for the classroom display or performance of a work, which are further extended for distance education by the TEACH Act, incorporated in the law in Appendix VIII.

Making photocopies for reserve collections is not expressly permitted under Section 108. As Laura Gasaway points out, "Traditional reserve collections in which only original volumes are placed into a special collection raise no copyright concerns for the library. [. . .] Copyright concerns arise only when materials are *reproduced* for library reserve collections" (Gasaway "Copyright Considerations" 113). Reproducing an item solely because it is in high demand is not a use permitted under Section 108.

However, if the Reserve Room is seen as an extension of the classroom rather than as a purely library operation (Harper, *Fair Use: Reserves* 119; Gasaway "Copyright Considerations"), then the classroom exemptions in the "Agreement on Guidelines for Classroom Copying in Not-For-Profit Educational Institutions with Respect to Books and Periodicals" can be applied (*Circular 21*, 7-8), as they were by the Conference on Fair Use (CONFU). Many librarians base their policies on some form of the CONFU guidelines (although they were never ratified by all the participants), or on the ALA Model Policy, which does not "represent negotiations between copyright holders and users," but is "merely the opinion of a library association" (Gasaway "Copyright Considerations" 119).

Most librarians feel that making photocopies for reserves constitutes a fair use under section 107 as well (Jackson 172). The University of Wisconsin at Madison, for example, bases its policy entirely on the fair use provisions without reference to other guidelines (http://steenbock. library.wisc.edu/reserves/copyrite.htm).

7. GUIDELINES (CONTU, CONFU)

In 1974, when Congress was beginning to work on the Copyright Act of 1976 in response to the innovation of widely available and reasonably priced photocopying, the National Commission on New Technological Uses of Copyrighted Works (CONTU) was formed to help develop definitions and guidelines relating to "systematic reproduction" in libraries. Subsection 108(g)(2) of the proposed Copyright Act placed limits on interlibrary loan, but allowed photocopying and sharing arrangements "that do not have, as their purpose or effect, that the library or archives receiving such copies or phonorecords for distribution does so in such aggregate quantities as to substitute for a subscription to or purchase of such work" (*CONTU Guidelines*, 2).

The original guidelines (*Circular 21*, 2-3; *CONTU Guidelines*) state that the following would constitute a "substitute for a subscription to or purchase of" a work:

- Six or more copies of one or more articles from the past five years of one journal title in a single calendar year
- Six or more copies of a section of a book, anthology, or collection in a single calendar year

Exceptions can be made if the library owns a copy of the work but it is not available for photocopying (for example, missing or long overdue) or if the item is on order. The various ALA Model Policies for interlibrary loan do not specify limits to the amount of material borrowed, referring the librarian to the copyright code and guidelines for information (http://www.cni.org/docs/infopols/ALA.html). The CONFU guidelines agreed with the CONTU borrowing limit of five article copies per year without permission fees ("the suggestion of five").

After these limits have been reached, the library should:

- Suggest the patron return after January 1st of the next year,
- Or purchase the item or a subscription to the journal,
- Or purchase the item from a document delivery service for the patron,
- Alternatively, seek permission from or pay royalties to the copyright holder.

The guidelines also state that records of all items borrowed must be kept for three full calendar years.

Other guidelines governing the use of copyrighted material by librarians and educators are collected in the United States Copyright Office's Circular 21, available online in PDF format at http://www.copyright. gov/circs/circ21.pdf. Of particular interest are the "Guidelines for Classroom Copying in Not-For-Profit Educational Institutions with Respect to Books and Periodicals." The sections on brevity, spontaneity and cumulative effect are especially applicable to reserves.

In the mid-1990s, the Conference on Fair Use (CONFU) attempted to create fair use guidelines similar to CONTU for electronic materials for interlibrary loan and reserves, but a consensus could not be reached between participants from the information producing industry and from the library and education world. As Georgia Harper reports, "Electronic Reserves negotiators were the most troubled group: their talks had broken down completely in the fall of 1995"; but as she points out, "the work performed by this group presents a valuable starting point for institutions wishing to develop their own electronic reserve guidelines" (Harper *CONFU*). The University of Texas System has used the CONFU guidelines in this way (http://www.utsystem.edu/ogc/intellectualproperty/copypol2.htm#rules) and other academic institutions have done so as well, "in the belief that they provide a reasonable framework for their electronic reserve operations" (Jackson 175).[2]

8. CONTRACTS vs. COPYRIGHT LAW: LICENSING AND UCITA

Electronic database and electronic journal subscriptions are obtained by contract rather than outright purchase. The library does not actually own the material, but pays only for access to it. Libraries sign licensing contracts setting out the terms of the agreement between the parties. When a library purchases a book or other physical work, in contrast, there is no need for a contract because the library's use of the material is governed by copyright law (although in some cases, as in annually leased reference works, a contract may be involved).

Contracts pose a problem because the terms proposed by the provider do not have to be in agreement with copyright law. This is especially disturbing when these contracts prohibit activities we have long considered to be fair use. By signing such a contract, we effectively agree to waive the fair use exceptions that our patrons expect to have. As Duane Webster explains:

> Routine library practices permitted under copyright law, such as interlibrary borrowing, lending for the classroom or at-home use by patrons, archiving, preservation and duplication for fair use purposes, have all been restricted, in some cases severely restricted and in other cases barred by licensing agreements. (Webster 3)

Fortunately, contracts are by their nature negotiable and libraries can try to negotiate favorable contracts that satisfy the needs of their patrons. A small library working alone may not have the leverage to negotiate exactly the terms it needs and may find it worthwhile to join a consortium for negotiating strength. On the other hand, as Georgia Harper has discovered, "very rarely do vendors refuse to negotiate their terms" (Harper *Acquisition* 1), so, it is always worthwhile to try. The library should examine carefully any clauses relating to interlibrary loan, electronic reserves, systematic copying, distribution, and linking to the database. The model licenses at http://www.licensingmodels.com/ provide sample clauses and definitions that can help libraries to rewrite licenses to allow interlibrary loan, electronic reserves and other uses (see Brennan, Hersey and Harper; Croft for additional advice on negotiating licenses).

The Uniform Computer Information Transactions Act (UCITA) is a proposal for a model state law that would make the terms of shrink-wrap or click-on software licenses more enforceable in states that adopt it. UCITA would permit producers to dictate terms prohibiting activities that are actually permitted by copyright law. Disturbingly, it would also allow the seller to withhold the terms of the contract until after the sale was made, and the contract may include clauses preventing the consumer from seeking any legal remedies if the software should prove to be defective or cause damage to their computer, as well as clauses that limit the use purchasers may make of materials they create using the software.

UCITA was opposed by a number of different consumer and educational organizations, among others, because it would be bad for consumers both directly, as purchasers of software and data, and indirectly, as users of libraries. Fortunately, the National Conference of Commissioners on Uniform State Laws (NCCUSL) has abandoned its efforts to formulate a version of UCITA acceptable to all parties and have it endorsed by the American Bar Association. Two states, Virginia and Maryland, have passed a version of UCITA, but several others have adopted "bomb-shelter" acts protecting their citizens from legal action under UCITA (Krause). Opponents of UCITA should not relax their guard, however, because powerful software manufacturer interests still desire the protections such an act would give them and may push for further action.

9. PENALTIES

If you, as a librarian, are charged with stepping over the bounds of fair use, what can you expect? There are two key concepts involved: *willful infringement* and *good faith*. Willful copyright infringement is a federal crime: if you willfully copy or distribute a work valued between $1,000 and $2,500, knowing that what you are doing is not a fair use, you could be fined and/or imprisoned. A copyright owner can sue for either actual or statutory damages; statutory damages are set at between $750 and $30,000 per infringement and the court can increase the damages up to $150,000 per infringement. However, as Mary Minow reassures us, "[I]f you work for a nonprofit education institution, library, or archives and are acting within the scope of employment the court can bring the statutory damage award down to *$0, even if you are found to be infringing copyright*. For this to happen, you must show that you believed and had reasonable grounds for believing that your use was Fair Use" (Minow 2). In other words, you must be able to prove that you made a good faith effort to adhere to the four factors of Fair Use before deciding to photocopy or scan the item. As Georgia Harper demonstrates, you should also be aware of your institution's policies on defending employees charged with copyright violations (Harper *Fair Use of Copyrighted Materials*).

Minow recommends that you analyze your use of each item and keep track of each analysis, using a tool such as Kenneth Crews' "Fair Use Checklist" (see Appendix 3). However, for a large library, it is impractical to document every photocopy or scan in this way. A more reasonable approach would be to develop strict internal guidelines, follow them religiously, review them frequently with all reserves department employees and occasionally spot-check a selection of items for adherence to these guidelines. In addition, reserve-room policies should make clear to instructors that they are expected to review their own requests for copyright compliance.

Educators preparing items for use in a classroom may find it advisable to consider filling out a checklist for each item, because they deal with a far smaller number of items and may be at greater risk for scrutiny than librarians. Anyone who writes for publication as part of their position should also consider reviewing their list of citations against this checklist.

NOTES

1. First sale rights can be limited if the material was never intended for public distribution. For example, in two cases materials intended only for distribution to church members have been removed from a library (*Hotaling v. Church of Jesus Christ of Latter-Day Saints*, 118 F 3rd 199 (4th Cir. 1997)) and from an Internet newsgroup (*Religious Technology Center v. NETCOM*, 907 F. Supp. 1361 (N.D. Cal. 1995)).

2. The CONFU guidelines apply primarily, though not exclusively, to book and journal excerpts and graphics (*Fair-Use Guidelines for Electronic Reserve Systems*, 1). Therefore, other agencies have developed guidelines suitable for formats other than text, notably music; see the Music Library Association's guidelines for reserves at http://www.lib.jmu.edu/Org/MLA/Guidelines/.

Chapter 2

Confidentiality Basics

1. STATE REGULATIONS

State law determines confidentiality of library patron records. Forty-eight states and the District of Columbia have confidentiality laws and the remaining two states (Hawaii and Kentucky) have opinions issued by their Attorneys General concerning privacy of library records. Every librarian should be familiar with the law in her state. Most states protect circulation and registration information, at a minimum. The American Library Association provides links to these state confidentiality statutes and opinions at: http://www.ala.org/Content/NavigationMenu/Our_ Association/Offices/Intellectual_Freedom3/IF_Groups_and_Committees/ State_IFC_Chairs/State_IFC_in_Action/State_Privacy_Laws_regarding_ Library_Records.htm.

2. INSTITUTIONAL REGULATIONS

Additionally, your parent institution may have statements or policies on confidentiality, particularly relating to computer use, which may be more or less stringent than state rules. Universities in particular often have regulations in place concerning who may request access to student records, including records of library use, and under what circumstances. Additionally, there may be policies about the circumstances under which the institution may examine a student's computer usage records,

[Haworth co-indexing entry note]: "Confidentiality Basics." Croft, Janet Brennan. Co-published simultaneously in *Journal of Interlibrary Loan, Document Delivery & Information Supply* (The Haworth Information Press, an imprint of The Haworth Press, Inc.) Vol. 14, No. 3, 2004, pp. 17-20; and: *Legal Solutions in Electronic Reserves and the Electronic Delivery of Interlibrary Loan* (Janet Brennan Croft) The Haworth Information Press, an imprint of The Haworth Press, Inc., 2004, pp. 17-20. Single or multiple copies of this article are available for a fee from The Haworth Document Delivery Service [1-800-HAWORTH, 9:00 a.m. - 5:00 p.m. (EST). E-mail address: docdelivery@haworthpress.com].

Digital Object Identifier: 10.1300/J110v14n03_03

for instance in a case where the University might find itself liable for a student's actions, as in recent Napster cases, where the parent institution has been held responsible for not taking steps to prevent illegal file-sharing (Heins "File Sharing" 1, 4). A librarian in a library within a larger parent institution should be familiar with any local policies.

The ALA Library Bill of Rights also supports confidentiality of patron records and while this is not a binding document, it does explore the ethical basis of protecting patron confidentiality and can provide a rationale for a library's policies if they are questioned. An updated discussion of this topic is available at http://www.ala.org/Content/NavigationMenu/Our_Association/ Offices/Intellectual_Freedom3/Statements_and_Policies/Intellectual_ Freedom2/Interpretations/Privacy.htm.

3. USA PATRIOT ACT

The USA PATRIOT Act, which was rapidly pushed through Congress in response to the terrorist attacks of 9/11/2001, supersedes local confidentiality regulations. This Act allows a subpoena or even immediate search and seizure of library records on the simple suspicion of a person's connection to terrorism and does not require a demonstration of probable cause in order to obtain the subpoena or search warrant from a judge. Additionally, librarians are subject to a gag order, which would prevent them from discussing any such request for records that might occur in their library, including any request that they might feel is an abuse of the Act. Another frightening aspect of the Act is that seizure of a library server would provide a law enforcement agency with access to all the library patron records stored on it, whether those patrons were under investigation or not, in effect permitting a "fishing expedition." While the concept of preventing terrorist acts through proactive measures seems reasonable, many people feel that the Act can too easily be used to violate individual rights.

Several new bills have recently been introduced in Congress to counteract certain provisions of the USA PATRIOT Act. On March 6, 2003, Representative Bernie Sanders (I-VT) introduced the "Freedom to Read Protection Act" (H.R. 1157), which would exempt library and bookseller records section 215 of the USA PATRIOT Act, which allows seizure of records without a warrant showing probable cause. Similar legislation, the "Library and Bookseller Protection Act" (S. 1158), was introduced by Senator Barbara Boxer (D-CA) in May 2003. Both would exempt libraries and booksellers from the "gag order" provision. The

"Library, Bookseller and Personal Records Privacy Act" (S.1507) was introduced by Senator Russell Feingold (D-WI) on July 31, 2003 and would set limits on the government's access to library, bookstore, medical and other personal information. The "Protecting the Rights of Individuals Act" (S.1552) was introduced on the same day by Senators Lisa Murkowski (R-AK) and Ron Wyden (D-OR) and includes several provisions relating to library patron confidentiality.

The national news media have frequently reported on the library community's concern over the USA PATRIOT Act and it has become a highly visible issue. While Attorney General John Ashcroft dismissed the American Library Association's concern as "hysterical" and claimed in September 2003 that the FBI has never used its power to request library patron records, an earlier report to Congress in May 2003 by the assistant attorney general indicated that the agency had visited at least 50 libraries (*In Wake of Declassified Report*).

A library's best means of protecting patron confidentiality is to develop and abide by a detailed records-retention policy and educate all staff about what is expected of them if they are approached with a search warrant or subpoena. As well, library administrators should encourage staff involvement in their state and national professional organizations' legislative committees.

4. RECORDS-RETENTION POLICIES

In response to the USA PATRIOT Act, many libraries have considered updating or revising their records retention policies. In the best interests of our patrons, many now think that records linking a patron to a particular item should be retained only as long as legitimately needed and all relevant statistics have been extracted, then removed from the system.

Under most circumstances it would take a certain amount of computer expertise to trace access to a particular Web page through IP addresses to a particular person, so most usage of a library's Web site is relatively confidential. Nevertheless, a typical electronic reserve system requires students to log in with an identifying user name and access to items might be traceable that way. A courseware system like Blackboard may provide managers with the capability of capturing information about who has accessed certain readings, although the list of potential readers is limited to registered students in that particular class. However, it is arguable that a class reading list is a public document; that reading the reserve items is expected of students enrolled in that class, just as reading the textbook is expected; that the list of students enrolled in a particular class is not privileged information; and that, therefore, whether a student accessed a particular document or not is either not protected information, or is a moot point, because he is presumed to have read it anyway as part of the class.

Interlibrary loan is a different situation. Under the copyright guidelines, records of items borrowed must be retained for three calendar years so that a library can analyze its borrowing patterns and purchase items or pay permission fees for those items for which they have gone beyond a fair number of borrowing requests. However, patron names need not be retained, so if records are kept in a format from which that field can easily be removed (such as in a spreadsheet program), then a records-retention policy might address stripping off the names as part of the process. Unfortunately, this might not entirely eradicate any record that a particular patron borrowed a particular item; OCLC retains records of transactions for six months and the lending library may retain records that include your patrons' names for an even longer period. You can be sure only that you are protecting the patrons at your end of the transaction, but that is no reason not to make every effort to do so.

Chapter 3

Electronic Reserves

1. ELECTRONIC vs. PHYSICAL RESERVES

How do electronic reserves differ from physical reserves? What are the legal implications of these differences? This section examines a list of differences and similarities between the traditional and electronic methods of delivering reserve materials and whether these differences change the way these methods are perceived legally.

A question to keep in mind is whether these differences are differences in kind, or just in scale. Do the two operations differ enough to justify tighter regulations for electronic reserve? Producers may find it disconcerting that an item is accessible 24 hours a day, 7 days a week, to multiple users simultaneously, any one of whom may possess the skill and desire to make the item available at touch of a button around the world. Nevertheless, is this truly different in kind from a patron faxing, or photocopying and mailing, an item to a large mailing list of friends, or just in scale? Moreover, is a difference in scale sufficient justification for tighter regulations?

On the other hand, electronic reserves can legitimately be seen as a very different kind of operation than physical reserves simply because of the technology involved. As the developers of the (unapproved) CONFU Guidelines pointed out:

> Making materials available through electronic reserve systems raises significant copyright issues. Electronic reserve operations include the

[Haworth co-indexing entry note]: "Electronic Reserves." Croft, Janet Brennan. Co-published simultaneously in *Journal of Interlibrary Loan, Document Delivery & Information Supply* (The Haworth Information Press, an imprint of The Haworth Press, Inc.) Vol. 14, No. 3, 2004, pp. 21-35; and: *Legal Solutions in Electronic Reserves and the Electronic Delivery of Interlibrary Loan* (Janet Brennan Croft) The Haworth Information Press, an imprint of The Haworth Press, Inc., 2004, pp. 21-35. Single or multiple copies of this article are available for a fee from The Haworth Document Delivery Service [1-800-HAWORTH, 9:00 a.m. - 5:00 p.m. (EST). E-mail address: docdelivery@haworthpress.com].

Digital Object Identifier: 10.1300/J110v14n03_04

making of a digital version of text, the distribution and display of that version at workstations, and downloading and printing of copies. (*Fair-Use Guidelines for Electronic Reserve Systems*, 1)

Jeff Rosedale has recently reassured information producers that "Nobody, not even the most cautious publisher, needs to lose any sleep over this natural extension of the library's role on campus" (Rosedale 182). Publishers do of course see this as a potential threat to their market; but since we were unable to agree on the CONFU guidelines, it is up to libraries to voluntarily develop policies to ensure that electronic reserves adhere to what we consider fair use of copyrighted material.

Location and Access

Traditionally, physical reserve items are set aside in a limited-access area of the library at faculty request or librarian's discretion. Generally, this is because of anticipated high use due to classroom assignment. Some items may be placed in a "permanent reserve" collection for protection, because of format, or because of general high use and/or susceptibility to theft, but technically these might be better-called "limited access" or "special collection" items than "reserve" items. Physical reserve collections date back to at least the late 1870s (Gasaway "Copyright Considerations" 111). A physical reserve collection may include items loaned by the instructor at his own risk, but they must meet fair use requirements if used without permission, just like any personal items he might use in the classroom.

For electronic reserve rooms, the items are duplicated in an electronic format (or may even be electronic from the start) and are made accessible over the Internet, generally through the library's Web page or through campus courseware. The same item may also be available physically in the library at the same time. The item might not even reside on the library's server; the library may simply provide a stable URL link to an item in a database or on the Internet. Electronic reserves started appearing in the 1990s, with the advent of the Internet (Jackson 169). Electronic reserves are almost exclusively material requested for a class by a professor; libraries have other ways of making digital material available to readers for other uses. As with physical reserves, electronic reserves may legally include items owned by the professor as well as by the library.

Copyright Implications

Both kinds of items are set aside in a special place, in one case physical and in the other electronic. Access to physical reserve items is generally looser, as in very few cases would a student have to prove he is enrolled in a certain class to access a reserve reading—and in fact reserve materials can often be borrowed and used by all classes of library users, not just students. This is not a copyright consideration when the item is the original, nor even when it is a physical photocopy, under the "Agreement on Guidelines for Classroom Copying" and sections 107 and 110. Although it is implied that the users of these items will be students of the instructor who placed them on reserve, it is not stated that these materials, therefore, have to be off-limits to other patrons.

Electronic reserve items require closer control. In practice, access is usually limited at its broadest to ID-holding members of the institution and in many cases to members of a specific class as well. The unapproved CONFU guidelines, which many libraries voluntarily use as a basis for their own policies, state that access should be limited strictly to students registered for the particular class and offer the following suggestions for achieving this:

- Individual password controls or verification of a student's registration status; or
- Password system for each class; or
- Retrieval of works by course number or instructor name, but not by author or title of the work; or
- Access limited to workstations that are ordinarily used by, or are accessible to, only enrolled students or appropriate staff or faculty (*Fair-Use Guidelines for Electronic Reserve Systems*).

The first two suggestions could be difficult to achieve with a homegrown system; the sophistication of a stand-alone system or a component of an integrated automation system would make compliance easier. In addition, the last suggestion would negate the advantage of electronic reserves for the student altogether. Mounting reserve readings on a campus courseware system is an option that would limit access to registered students only, but which raises confidentiality questions. The third suggestion is the easiest option for a library developing a homegrown system.

Classification

Physical reserve items may be arranged on the shelf by name of professor, number of course, call number, etc., in whatever way is most convenient for the library staff. Generally, items are also accessible through some form of catalog or index (online, card, three-ring binder, etc.), by at least one access point in addition to the shelf arrangement (professor, course number, title, etc.). A physical reserve system that is a component of an integrated library automation system may display reserve items and their location in the regular online catalog, facilitating access for library users not enrolled in the particular class and providing numerous access points per record.

With the typical software available for electronic reserves (either commercial or home grown), students find their assigned readings by locating their course or professor on a list or menu. With the more sophisticated systems, the student sees only the courses in which he is enrolled. Generally, no other access point is available to students, although administrators and instructors may have more access points or search capabilities.

Copyright Implications

Since use of an electronic reserve item should ideally be restricted to the students in that class only, providing classification access only through class number is sufficient for students and is recommended by CONFU guidelines. Instructors and staff are exempt from these restrictions, so allowing them additional searching methods is permissible (*Fair-Use Guidelines for Electronic Reserve Systems*, 3). For library-owned items, the original is still accessible to other library users by other methods than going through the reserve system, so no other access point is necessary for patrons not in the particular class.

Circulation

Students must generally request a physical item in person at the reserve desk and the item, if available, is immediately signed out to that person. Items can sometimes be renewed, or recalled from another patron, depending on local policies. Items may or may not be permitted to leave the building. Since the library owns the item or the photocopy and is only lending it to the student, it is not distributing it, as no change of ownership occurs and thus this is a fair use (Gasaway "Copyright Considerations" 113-4).

Typically, a student enters an electronic reserves page through the library's Web page and then types in a user name and password to access his readings. Depending on the sophistication of the software, he may need to choose a department and course or an instructor's name from a menu, or he may be presented with a list of the courses in which he is enrolled. The process is entirely self-serve. There is no need for renewals or recalls, because any number of students can access the item simultaneously for as long as they wish.

Copyright Implications

In this case, there is a clear difference of kind. Circulation of a physical item is treated as a loan, even if the student is merely borrowing the item long enough to take it to the nearest photocopier. When he does, it is wholly his responsibility to adhere to the copyright regulations posted by the photocopier; the library is not responsible if he does not (*Copyright Law of the United States*, 108(f)(1)). With an electronic reserve system, the student is assumed to be acquiring a copy, either physical or digital, of the item. It is assumed he will not just read the item from the computer screen and move on. The library has a certain responsibility to adhere to 108(a) and 108(d) regarding supplying a copy to a patron, in addition to the patron's own responsibility about what he does with his copy. (See the section on copying for further discussion.)

Use of Service

Students who never enter the library for any other reason might come in for an assigned physical reserve reading. This is an opportunity to attract them to other library services. Similarly, students who never use the library's Web site for any other reason may use it for an assigned reading. Again, this is an opportunity to attract them to other Web-based library services.

Copyright Implications

The CONFU guidelines make it clear that students "should not be charged specifically or directly for access to electronic reserve systems" (*Fair-Use Guidelines for Electronic Reserve Systems*, 3). The earlier "ALA Model Policy Concerning College and University Photocopying for Classroom, Research and Library Reserve Use" also made it clear that students should not be "assessed any fee beyond the actual cost of the photocopying" (cited Gasaway *Copyright Law Course Materials* 35). This is clear and easy to comply with.

However, under section 108(a), libraries also cannot make any *indirect* profit from copying and still claim fair use. If there is any possibility that the library can be construed as a for-profit institution, then attracting students to other (possibly profit-making) services could be seen as ethically questionable by an information producer. A library at a for-profit educational institution might be considered as inseparable from its parent institution and therefore unable to offer either electronic reserves or photocopied physical reserves without seeking permission for every single item;

such a library should consult with its institution's legal counsel about its status.

Access in Time

Physical reserves are usually given a limited loan period. This makes them useful only to traditional on-campus students or local, daily commuters. On the other hand, electronic reserves are available at any time from the privacy of a student's own computer. This, of course, makes electronic reserves invaluable for distance education, but it is a boon for traditional on-campus and commuter students as well.

Copyright Implications

None of the guidelines advise libraries about a standard loan period for physical reserve materials; as far as the guidelines are concerned, the loan period could last as long as the semester for which the reading is assigned. Electronic reserve items do not have an actual loan period by their very nature. However, for both types, reserve access is usually limited to a single semester: most guidelines state that an instructor cannot keep the same item on reserve for two semesters in a row.

Keeping an item on reserve for students who earned an "incomplete" and need to finish a course later is problematic, but easier to justify with electronic reserves, where the material will still be restricted to students in that class and where the original is still available to other library users. The CONFU guidelines do in fact allow for this situation (*Fair-Use Guidelines for Electronic Reserve Systems*, 3).

Access in Space

Physical items can be used by only one borrower at a time and can be borrowed only when the library is open. Often reserves are not allowed to leave the library building. As with restrictions in time, this makes them useful only to traditional on-campus students or local commuters. On the other hand, with electronic reserves, many students may access the same document at the same time, from any location. Again, this makes electronic reserves invaluable for both distance education and traditional on-campus or commuter students.

Copyright Implications

In the case of electronic reserves, no library employee is present to physically verify that the user has a valid ID, which brings up the possibility that someone off-campus might hack into the reserve system and download files which should be restricted to students. Adequate control over the ID and password system should help to prevent this.

Patron Records

Physical reserves are generally checked out using the same circulation system as other library items, or at least one that is similar. The library creates records showing which student has borrowed which items and when they are due back. The amount of time these records are retained varies from library to library. Some libraries also permit professors to have access to records of which students used their reserve items, or attach a sign-in sheet to the item itself, although this is controversial and may or may not be considered a violation of patron confidentiality. As mentioned above, it may be possible to argue that the list of students participating in a given class is not confidential (and certainly not unknown to the professor), nor is the list of reading material for that class, and that all students might reasonably be presumed to have read the reserve material.[1] Nevertheless, whether this information will actually be of use to the instructor is another question; a sign-in sheet will not reflect those cases in which a student lent his photocopy to other students in the class.

A library generally does not automatically keep a record of which patron has accessed which electronic reserve document, although some systems may allow this information to be extracted. If the library uses campus courseware to mount reserve readings, a professor or teaching assistant associated with the course may be able to tell which students have accessed which readings. A library considering using courseware to mount reserve readings will want to consider patron confidentiality and whether it should apply to course reserves or not. As with physical reserves, it is questionable both whether this information is privileged from the instructor and whether it will serve as an accurate record of which students have done the readings.

Confidentiality Implications

A strict interpretation of confidentiality statutes would recommend that a records-retention policy should be developed for reserve circulation, but there are valid arguments for allowing instructors access to information on who has borrowed or accessed reserve items.

Copying

A physical reserve collection may contain single or multiple copies of an individual item (if the "Guidelines on Classroom Copying" are taken as applying to library reserves, then there is an upper limit of one copy of each item per student). It is not expected to be a substitute for buying a textbook or a course pack, because the instructor is supposed to place only a limited portion of the required readings on reserve without permission and the library is not giving away or selling their copies and provides only limited loan periods. However, students may photocopy reserve items at their own expense, although they are responsible for staying within the copyright code that should be posted at every library photocopier. This can make physical reserves appear to function as a copy-it-yourself textbook or course pack.

With electronic reserves, creating a copy of the document for later reading is simpler and cheaper for the user. He can print it on a library or computer lab printer for a fee, or at home for the cost of paper and ink, or he may be able to e-mail it to himself or save it to a disk or hard drive, depending on the format and his software. In this way e-reserves may appear to function as a low-cost, user-printed alternative to a textbook or course pack, which is why the CONFU guidelines state that only a small proportion of the assigned reading for any course should be placed on electronic reserve without permission (*Fair-Use Guidelines for Electronic Reserve Systems*, 2).

Copyright Implications

The ease of printing or saving electronic reserves and the possibility of sharing and distributing the readings outside of class are the major concerns of copyright holders. It has always been possible to share a physical item by making and mailing multiple copies; even before photocopiers, there were mimeograph machines, typewriters and carbon paper, or plain old copying by hand!

Therefore, this is more a difference of scale than of kind. However, the difference in scale is enormous. With electronic sharing, there is no decrease in quality as the item is copied; the copy is for all intents and purposes identical to the original, and it costs the user nothing to distribute a copy to either one or one million friends. Additionally, the patron who makes photocopies and mails them out is the only one responsible for his violation of fair use (if any); but with electronic reserves, the library may also be implicated if it originally posts an item that is not used fairly and if it does not take some steps to limit access to the item.

Though it costs the consumer more to photocopy and snail mail an item he wants to share than to scan or download and e-mail it, both methods earn the producer nothing. It would be hard to prove that they cost the producer anything, either, which is why a producer may choose to sue for statutory damages rather than actual damages. Therefore, a library must be careful to make illegal distribution as difficult as possible, as an act of good faith. Each item should include a copy of the standard copyright caution, as recommended in the CONFU guidelines, which prohibits further distribution of the item (*Fair-Use Guidelines for Electronic Reserve Systems*, 2-3).

Scanning a document to create a .PDF file, rather than posting a .DOC file, will make it more difficult to cut and paste portions into an e-mail for distribution; forcing the user to send it as an attached file will place some limits on his ability to distribute it and preserve the integrity of the document as well. (Plagiarism is outside of the scope of this book, but this also helps eliminate cut-and-paste copying into student papers.)

The Digital Millennium Copyright Act also implies, but does not clearly state, that any attempt to circumvent library measures to prevent downloading and distributing e-reserve items would be against the law.

2. DEVELOPING AN ELECTRONIC RESERVES LEGAL POLICY

What should go in an e-reserve legal and copyright policy? Because of the lack of consensus about e-reserves and the fact that inter-library cooperation and standardization is not an issue, this is more complicated than developing an interlibrary loan policy.

Subsequent Semesters

This is a subject open to much debate, and at this point it seems each institution should make its own decision, based on its understanding of the law and the technology available to it, and be prepared to justify its policies if necessary.

CONFU guidelines suggest that an item cannot be used in "a subsequent academic term" for the same course offered by the same instructor, or by multiple sections of the same class taught by different instructors during the same semester, without paying permission fees (*Fair-Use*

Guidelines for Electronic Reserve Systems, 3). In the "Guidelines on Classroom Copying," section III(C)(c) says that copying should not "be repeated with respect to the same item by the same teacher from term to term" (see Appendix 1).

However, should "subsequent" refer to the next semester only, or to any later semester? The "ALA Model Policy Concerning College and University Photocopying for Classroom, Research and Library Use," in contrast to the CONFU guidelines, says only that "the distribution of the same photocopied material [should] not occur *every* semester" (cited Gasaway, *Copyright Law Course Materials* 35-6, emphasis added), implying that simply skipping a semester ensures fair use for physical reserves, at least.

A number of university e-reserve policies state that an item can be used only one semester, period, without permission. For an example, see the University of Kentucky (http://www.uky.edu/Libraries/Reserves/guidelines.html). These libraries interpret fair use more narrowly, feeling that it would violate the general intent of the guidelines for both reserves and classroom teaching if an item was used again for the same class a year later. Using the same item again would violate the principle of spontaneity that is part of the "Guidelines for Classroom Copying." This is a reasonable reading of the regulations.

However, unless a library keeps detailed and extensive records of every item ever put on electronic reserve, including the name of the professor and the course and semester he used it for, and checks each incoming item against these records for a match in all categories, it would be impossible to make sure there were no such violations of the spirit of the law. If a library does not keep such records, it has no way to enforce a one-semester-only policy, other than relying on the good will of the instructors.

Storage

When the CONFU guideline states that an item may be stored digitally until the next academic term it is needed, it implies that it may be acceptable to skip a semester and use the item again without seeking permission (*Fair-Use Guidelines for Electronic Reserve Systems*, 3). Will the library store materials for instructors if they will be used again after an intervening semester? Does the library prefer not to do this, in case an intervening semester is not enough to ensure fair use? On the other hand, will the library require permission before a stored item can be used again?

Many library policies simply state that all reserve materials will be removed at the end of each semester and do not mention reusing materials in a succeeding semester. For example, the University of Colorado policy simply states that "electronic files cannot be archived for future use," but does not specifically prohibit any future use (http://lib.colostate.edu/access/ereserve/ERcopyrightpolicy.pdf). On the other hand, The Lilly Library at Duke University specifically suggests that instructors save their hard copies for future re-scanning for use another semester (http://www.lib.duke.edu/lilly/facultyreserves.html). Most libraries will prefer not to take on the burden of storing documents at the end of the semester, whether they expect to post them again or not.

Limited Access

Who will have access to the reserve readings? The CONFU guidelines suggest that access should be limited as much as possible to students in the class for which the readings are assigned and to their instructor and library staff members. However, the guidelines by necessity leave the technical means up to the individual institution, offering only a few suggestions.

How will access be limited? A library without a sophisticated IT department to call upon may find it impossible to create a secure e-reserves environment and should consider limiting electronic reserve readings only to public domain items, as it would be both unethical and extremely risky to post copyrighted items without a method to restrict access.

A slightly more technologically advanced institution, without the resources to purchase a system designed to handle e-reserves, may still be able to limit access by tying into the university personnel database and requiring ID and password access. However, without some filtering mechanism, all university students, faculty and staff may be able to access reserve readings. This still offers some level of protection against prosecution, as e-reserves are not available to the public. If the library is also able to implement one of the various CONFU suggestions for limiting access, possibly by its choice of organization and classification scheme for the readings, this may be a comfortable compromise.

In any case, a library should be prepared to defend its policies and procedures if it cannot afford or develop a system that will restrict access to readings only to students in that class.

Confidentiality of Patron Records

The library should decide on how strictly to enforce confidentiality of patron records for reserves. Should records be confidential from instructors? If the library wishes to use a campus-wide courseware system that allows instructors to see which readings their students have accessed, is this a compromise the library is prepared to justify to the students? Does the library feel that students should be warned that their instructors might be able to access records of what items they have looked at for that particular class?

Copyright Warning

How will the copyright warning be worded? Will it appear as a separate cover page? Will it be stamped on each page of an item before scanning, or just the first page? Will there also be a notice in the explanatory material on the reserve room homepage? Does the copyright warning make responsibility for infringement clear and match the parent institution's policies? The ALA Model Policy requires a copyright notice on the first page of any photocopied item (cited Gasaway *Copyright Law Course Materials* 35) and the CONFU guidelines suggest a warning on a preliminary or introductory screen (*Fair-Use Guidelines for Electronic Reserve Systems*, 2).

Responsibility for Seeking Permissions

Is the library or the instructor responsible for seeking permission to put an item on reserve? What documents does the library expect from the instructor, if he is responsible? Who will be held responsible if there is a problem with the permission?

Library Portion of Permission Fees

Will the library pay all, none, a portion, or a percentage of permission fees if required? On the other hand, is the instructor or his department responsible? A 1999 ARL study indicated that most libraries do not pay these fees out of their own budget (cited Jackson 178).

Use While Seeking Permissions

Is the library willing to put the item on reserve while permission is being sought, knowing that the item may have to be removed in mid-semester? The CONFU guidelines suggest that this is permissible for up to three years, but these guidelines were written in 1996. Online permissions sources, like Copyright Clearance Center, have streamlined the process since that time and a shorter period, like one year, might be more reasonable.

What will the library do if no copyright owner is found–continue to use the item or remove it? Canadian librarians are fortunate to be able to obtain an "unlocatable copyright owner" license that will allow them to use a work for five years (http://www.cb-cda.gc.ca/unlocatable/index-e.html), but American librarians do not have this option and will have to assess the risks of continuing to use the item.

Limits on Amount of Material from Each Title, Etc.

The ALA Model Policy restates the Fair Use principle that the effect of the use should not be detrimental to the market for the work (cited Gasaway *Copyright Law Course Materials* 35-6). The "Guidelines for Classroom Copying" (see Appendix 1) offer some very specific guidelines for how much material can be copied for classroom distribution and the CONFU guidelines also include some more general definitions (*Fair-Use Guidelines for Electronic Reserve Systems*, 2). Libraries may want to create limits comparable to these guidelines and to those used at peer institutions.

Explaining Copyright to Instructors

The selection of items to be placed on reserve for professors is subject to the four factors of fair use set out in Section 108 of the copyright law and the regulations on classroom use from section 110, as well as the guidelines reproduced on pages 7-8 of Circular 21. The library should provide some guidance for instructors that will help them determine if their intended use is fair.

In the best interests of the larger institution, the library should make every effort to make the electronic reserve process easy to understand and to make compliance as simple as possible, in order to encourage instructors to use the e-reserve system. When instructors use the library's system, library staff can oversee compliance with copyright. This saves instructors from running the risks of placing material on their own Web pages, which may not meet fair use requirements and may not be off-limits to outsiders. This situation could create a liability not just for the instructor but also for the institution as a whole.

3. NEGOTIATING PERMISSIONS
FOR ELECTRONIC RESERVE USE

The Copyright Clearance Center provides permissions for both physical and electronic reserves and sophisticated tools for managing permissions requests. Publishers may be more reluctant to allow use of their materials for electronic reserves than physical reserves and have been known to charge "such high royalties that they in effect deny permission for use" (Gasaway "Copyright Considerations" 128). For non-print and international permissions, see the resources listed in Appendix 3.

4. NEGOTIATING DATABASE CONTRACTS TO PROVIDE FOR ELECTRONIC RESERVE USE

Whether or not a library can fulfill some electronic reserve needs by using material from the electronic databases to which it subscribes is determined by the database contract, not by fair use or other guidelines. The license may permit the library to print and scan an item for reserve use, or link directly to an item, or prohibit use for reserves altogether. Whether it is technically feasible to link to an item may depend on whether the database is accessible when the student is signed in to the electronic reserve system. It is advisable for libraries to consider their electronic reserves needs when negotiating or renewing a license and libraries may find it useful to be familiar with the wording found in model licenses when negotiating (Croft 168).

5. CASES

According to Laura Gasaway's chapter in the 2002 collection *Managing Electronic Reserves*, there has been no litigation to date over electronic reserves, nor any reported cease and desist orders (Gasaway "Copyright Considerations" 128). Music librarians have also been fortunate that their use of streaming audio to offer assigned listening on electronic reserve has not been challenged in the courts (Gasaway "Copyright Considerations" 130), although music librarians may be wise to keep a close watch on developments in the recent RIAA suits against music downloaders.

But there are several cases related to the issues involved in e-reserves:

- *Basic Books v. Kinko's*, 758 F. Supp. 1522 (S.D.N.Y. 1991) on course pack copying
- *Princeton University Press v. Michigan Documents Service*, 99 F. 3d 1381 (6th Cir. 1996) on course pack copying
- *American Geophysical Union v. Texaco, Inc.*, 60 F 3rd 913, 923 (2nd Cir. 1994) on for-profit libraries and on the article as an entire work rather than a portion of a work.

Summaries of these cases and other important fair use and copyright cases can be found at the Stanford University Libraries Copyright and Fair Use Site: http://fairuse.stanford.edu/primary_materials/cases/index.html.

6. CURRENT LEGISLATIVE ISSUES

TEACH Act

The TEACH Act sets forth the conditions under which instructors in non-profit institutions can use copyrighted materials in distance education. It applies only to material that an instructor would present during a class session and not to supplementary material that might include textbooks, course packs, or library reserves.

UCITA

Librarians involved with electronic reserves should keep an eye on UCITA developments in their state, since UCITA would make the terms of shrink-wrap or click-on licenses enforceable over fair use and may mean some materials currently usable for e-reserves would be off-limits.

DMCA

The most likely effect of DMCA is that more and more works will be published digitally with stronger limitations on what libraries can use them for without negotiating contracts to include electronic reserves.

NOTE

1. Although, of course, this does not always happen! Laura Gasaway cites a study on physical reserves showing that only 40% of the students in a class actually borrowed the reserve items and this does not mean they read them (Gasaway, "Copyright Considerations" 112).

Chapter 4

Electronic Delivery of Interlibrary Loan

1. ELECTRONIC vs. PHYSICAL DELIVERY OF INTERLIBRARY LOAN

How does electronic delivery of interlibrary loan articles differ from traditional physical delivery and what are the legal implications? Does electronic delivery of interlibrary loan constitute a difference in kind or scale? As with electronic reserves, we will look at a list of similarities and differences between traditional and electronic delivery of interlibrary loan items and examine the legal implications.

Photocopying for interlibrary loan use is implied in the copyright law in sections 108(d) and 108(e), which discuss a user requesting a copy "made from the collection of a library or archives where the user makes his or her request or from that of another library or archives." The CONTU guidelines go into far greater detail and, as they are approved as part of the copyright code and are included in Circular 21, there is far less ambiguity about what is permitted and forbidden for interlibrary loan than for reserves.

There are several issues concerning interlibrary loan addressed in the copyright law and guidelines:

* Libraries cannot substitute interlibrary loan for purchasing an item
* Libraries cannot profit directly or indirectly from interlibrary loan (any fees must be for cost recovery only)
* A copy must become the property of the user

[Haworth co-indexing entry note]: "Electronic Delivery of Interlibrary Loan." Croft, Janet Brennan. Co-published simultaneously in *Journal of Interlibrary Loan, Document Delivery & Information Supply* (The Haworth Information Press, an imprint of The Haworth Press, Inc.) Vol. 14, No. 3, 2004, pp. 37-44; and: *Legal Solutions in Electronic Reserves and the Electronic Delivery of Interlibrary Loan* (Janet Brennan Croft) The Haworth Information Press, an imprint of The Haworth Press, Inc., 2004, pp. 37-44. Single or multiple copies of this article are available for a fee from The Haworth Document Delivery Service [1-800-HAWORTH, 9:00 a.m. - 5:00 p.m. (EST). E-mail address: docdelivery@haworthpress.com].

http://www.haworthpress.com/web/JILIS
Digital Object Identifier: 10.1300/J110v14n03_05

- The library must have no notice that the user plans to use it for any purpose other than private study, scholarship, or research
- The officially worded warning about copyright compliance must be posted where orders are taken and on the order form
- The library must not perform any "systematic" copying for ILL.

Location and Access

Physical interlibrary loan items, whether originals or photocopies, are generally picked up at a specific location within the library, unless the library is willing to deliver the item to the borrower. "Returnables," or books and other original items like microfilm, must leave their home library, which is risky but unavoidable, for items too lengthy to photocopy.

Photocopies and electronic delivery allow returnables to stay safely at their home library, if the excerpt needed is short enough to copy or scan. Typically, electronic delivery of interlibrary loan documents involves the lending library scanning a physical item and sending the scan to the borrowing library. The borrowing library then passes the item on to the patron by posting it on a secure Web site for a limited amount of time, where the patron can access it with a password a limited number of times. The contract for an electronic database may permit using items from the database for interlibrary loan by printing and scanning the item, copying the item electronically and sending it as a file, or some other method. On the other hand, it may prohibit using the database for interlibrary loan altogether.

Copyright Implications

Lending a returnable item is a simple application of the first sale doctrine. Sending a photocopy is also fairly straightforward, as section 108(d)(1) allows a library to supply a user with a copy of an item from his library "or another library or archives," as long as the copy becomes his property, he gives no indication that the item will be used for any other than "private study, scholarship, or research," and the copyright notice is clearly displayed at the place where his order was taken. Sending a digital copy has been seen as more problematic, since technically the lending library makes a digital copy in the process of scanning it and the borrowing library makes a digital copy in the process of receiving it. However, the lending library's copy is only a by-product of the process and is always discarded or deleted immediately. The borrowing library keeps its digital copy posted only long enough to ensure that the patron has had an opportunity to view it, and then it is deleted as well.

Circulation

Physical interlibrary loan items are usually picked up at a certain place in the library. Returnables are checked out to the borrower for a certain period based on the date the item is due back to the lending library and usually may be renewed. Non-returnables (photocopies) become the property of the borrower, as required by law. The library may make temporary records for returnables in its own circulation system, or keep interlibrary loan lending records separate.

Electronic interlibrary loan documents are usually posted on the Web site for only a brief period, allowing the user sufficient time to access and print or download the item, then removed. If the borrower prints out the item, it becomes his property, just as a copy supplied physically by the library would be.

Copyright Implications

The document should be accessible only to the person who requested it, or it might be perceived as systematic copying and distribution of an article. It should be kept on the library's server for only a limited time, or it could imply that the library has borrowed the material in lieu of purchasing it.

Use of Service

Interlibrary loan is not usually an entry-level service; knowledgeable and motivated patrons seek it out. When electronic interlibrary loan ordering is offered, the service may become more visible to the average library Web site visitor and use may increase.

Copyright Implications

As with electronic reserves, interlibrary loan should operate only on a cost-recovery basis, since a library should make neither a direct nor an indirect profit from supplying photocopies. A library that is part of a for-profit institution should check with its legal counsel, because this service may be seen as something designed to lead users on to profit-making library or other institutional services. A library in this situation may need to request permission for every item it borrows, rather than anything over the "suggestion of five."

Patron Records

The borrowing process requires extensive records on borrowed items, including records of who requested the item. It is especially important to keep records on returnable items until they have made it back to their home library safely, which means records of when the item was picked up and when it was returned. With non-returnable items and electronic items, there is no need to keep patron records once the item has been picked up, unless the library needs them for statistical purposes.

Confidentiality Implications

Libraries are required to keep records on their borrowing for three calendar years, so that they can check for compliance with the "suggestion of five" and pay any necessary permission fees. However, there is no requirement to keep patron records as well. If a library wishes to track interlibrary loan borrowing by department or user type, that information is already collected in specific fields on the interlibrary loan form, so the name field could be deleted, leaving this information in place.

Copying

For as long as there have been photocopiers, users of interlibrary loan have been able to copy and mail the items they borrow to friends and colleagues. Nevertheless, as with electronic reserves, information providers are wary of one-touch dissemination to large groups of people by the recipient of an electronic interlibrary loan document. The user can print the item, save it to a disc or hard drive, or possibly send it to one or ten thousand friends via e-mail or by posting on the Internet. Digital copies never degrade, no matter how many times they are recopied, and they cost nothing to send to either one or one million other e-mail addresses.

Technology makes such a great difference that it becomes a difference in kind and not just in scale.

Copyright Implications

The owner of the copy is ultimately responsible for adhering to copyright law, not the supplying library. Our responsibilities include posting the appropriate copyright warning forms at the place where orders are taken, on the order form, on the document, and at our photocopiers; and refusing a loan if the patron informs us it will be used for a purpose other than private study, scholarship, or research. Since the copy is owned by the patron rather than lent by the library, responsibility for copyright compliance rests with him.

2. DEVELOPING AN INTERLIBRARY LOAN LEGAL POLICY

What should go into an interlibrary loan legal and copyright policy?

The Suggestion of Five

The library should follow the "suggestion of five" from the CONTU Guidelines and request permission for usage beyond these limits. These limits should be included or referred to in the policy, so that patrons will be aware there may be reasons we might not be able to request an item they want.

Secure Delivery System

Items should be accessible only to the patron, for a limited amount of time.

Confidentiality of Records

A record-retention policy should address removing patron names as soon as a returnable item is received at its home library, or as soon as a non-returnable is picked up.

Copyright Notices

Where will the library place its copyright notices? Notices are required at several locations:

- At the place where orders are taken. Required wording shown below. Location, font and paper weight are specified in 37 CFR 201.14 (http://www.copyright.gov/title37/201/37cfr201-14.html).
- On the order form, including electronic order forms. Same wording as above. Moreover, see 37 CFR 201.14 for details on how it is to be printed on the order form.

- On the document. At a minimum, must say "This material may be protected by copyright" (Crews 127). For further discussion, see http://www.copyright.iupui.edu/super_copying.htm.
- At each public photocopier in the library (no particular wording is mandated, but many library supply catalogs carry standardized signs with wording suggested by ALA).

This is the wording for the required notice:

Notice: Warning Concerning Copyright Restrictions

The copyright law of the United States (Title 17, United States Code) governs the making of photocopies or other reproductions of copyrighted material.

Under certain conditions specified in the law, libraries and archives are authorized to furnish a photocopy or other reproduction. One of these specific conditions is that the photocopy or reproduction is not to be "used for any purpose other than private study, scholarship, or research." If a user makes a request for, or later uses, a photocopy or reproduction for purposes in excess of "fair use," that user may be liable for copyright infringement.

This institution reserves the right to refuse to accept a copying order if, in its judgment, fulfillment of the order would involve violation of copyright law.

Fees

Under section 108 (a), libraries may charge fees only for cost-recovery for a use to remain fair use. OCLC encourages its member libraries to use Interlibrary Loan Fee Management (IFM), which tracks fees libraries charge each other and manages deposit accounts and credits. Individual libraries must decide how much, if any, of these fees will be passed on to the patron.

3. NEGOTIATING PERMISSIONS FOR INTERLIBRARY LOAN USE

Will the library set up a deposit account arrangement with the Copyright Clearance Center, or just seek permissions on an as-needed basis? What if permission is sought but there is no response? Will the library borrow the item anyway? Gilmer cites a suggestion that the letter requesting permission include a statement that the copy will be made unless a reply forbidding the copying is received within a certain length of time (Gilmer 88). What will the library do if the copyright holder cannot be located?

4. NEGOTIATING DATABASE CONTRACTS FOR INTERLIBRARY LOAN USE

The database contract, rather than fair use, determines if items in an electronic database or from an electronic journal can be used to fill interlibrary loan requests. A license may allow direct electronic transmission of a document; it may require the document to be printed and then scanned and transmitted by fax or e-mail; it may permit only physical printed copies to be sent via regular mail; or it may forbid interlibrary loan altogether (Croft and Murphy 7-8). Since contracts are by their nature negotiable, a library's best approach would be to develop an interlibrary loan clause describing exactly what it wishes to be able to do in order to fill interlibrary loan requests from the database and then use this as a basis for negotiation. Model licenses, such as those listed on the LIBLICENSE-L Web site (http://www.library.yale.edu/~llicense), are designed to help libraries develop wording for the clauses they wish to renegotiate. Many databases are acquired through consortia and this would be a good approach for consortia negotiators to take as well.

5. CASES

- *Williams & Wilkins v. National Library of Medicine*, 487 F. 2d. 1345 (Ct. Cl. 1973), affirmed 420 U.S. 376 (1975). An interlibrary loan case before the Copyright Act of 1976.
- *Tasini v. The New York Times Co.*, 192 F.3d 356 (2nd Cir. 1999) amended 206 F.3rd 161, affirmed 533 U.S. 483 (2001). Articles copyrighted by a freelance author were included in the NYT electronic databases, without compensation to the author. May lead to the withdrawal of freelance-authored items from many databases.
- *Ryan v. Carl Corporation*, 23 F. Supp. 2d 1146 (N.D. Cal. 1998). Freelance authors found their works were being distributed by Carl's UnCover (a for-profit document delivery service) without their permission being sought and their publishers were being paid instead. *Ryan v. Carl* is unlikely to lead to any action against nonprofit libraries.

6. CURRENT LEGISLATIVE ISSUES

UCITA

If UCITA were to be passed, database clauses forbidding use of their contents for interlibrary loan would become more enforceable in that particular state. Librarians involved with interlibrary loan should keep an eye on attempts to introduce UCITA in their states. It is possible that UCITA will also affect interlibrary loan across state lines, if one state has passed UCITA and another has not.

USA PATRIOT Act

Patron records for both borrowing and lending could be subpoenaed under the Patriot Act. Libraries should consider developing records retention policies for interlibrary loan, which retain the essential information about each transaction but eliminate the patron names.

Chapter 5

Conclusion

Time and experience will show that the publisher-librarian controversy over copyright, interlibrary loan and photocopying was the result of fear and misunderstanding–largely on the part of the publishers.

–Lois C. Gilmer

Similar copyright issues affect both electronic reserves and electronic delivery of interlibrary loan documents. In both cases, publishers and producers fear a loss of profit through widespread and unauthorized distribution of their products. Authors have concerns about their control over their own work as well. Sometimes libraries are seen as the enemy, encouraging indiscriminate free access to materials–no better than the developers of file sharing systems. There is no question that our patrons want and will use these services if they are available. It is in our best interests to be proactive in developing guidelines based at heart on the four factors of Fair Use and acceptable to as many parties as possible without compromising these principles.

Fair Use is an essential balancing principle at the core of copyright law in this country and the basis of our service. Our voluntary adherence to widely available guidelines, even if they are not approved by all publishers and producers, signals our good faith efforts to respect the rights of copyright holders while still advocating the broadest interpretation we can of Fair Use factors.

[Haworth co-indexing entry note]: "Conclusion." Croft, Janet Brennan. Co-published simultaneously in *Journal of Interlibrary Loan, Document Delivery & Information Supply* (The Haworth Information Press, an imprint of The Haworth Press, Inc.) Vol. 14, No. 3, 2004, pp. 45-46; and: *Legal Solutions in Electronic Reserves and the Electronic Delivery of Interlibrary Loan* (Janet Brennan Croft) The Haworth Information Press, an imprint of The Haworth Press, Inc., 2004, pp. 45-46. Single or multiple copies of this article are available for a fee from The Haworth Document Delivery Service [1-800-HAWORTH, 9:00 a.m. - 5:00 p.m. (EST). E-mail address: docdelivery@haworthpress.com].

Digital Object Identifier: 10.1300/J110v14n03_06

The author is not a lawyer and recommends that you seek the advice of your institution's counsel when in doubt concerning your particular situation. It is also recommended that you and other members of your library staff become involved with your state and national professional associations' legislative committees and work to educate lawmakers about library issues and concerns.

Appendix 1

Copyright Law

Below are reproduced in their entirety the texts of sections 107, 108 and 109 and portions of 110 of the Copyright Law; the Guidelines for Classroom Copying; the CONTU Guidelines for Interlibrary Loan; the unapproved CONFU Guidelines on Electronic Reserves; and portions of the ALA Model Policy on Photocopying.

§ 107. Limitations on Exclusive Rights: Fair Use

Notwithstanding the provisions of sections 106 and 106A, the fair use of a copyrighted work, including such use by reproduction in copies or phonorecords or by any other means specified by that section, for purposes such as criticism, comment, news reporting, teaching (including multiple copies for classroom use), scholarship, or research, is not an infringement of copyright. In determining whether the use made of a work in any particular case is a fair use the factors to be considered shall include—

(1) The purpose and character of the use, including whether such use is of a commercial nature or is for nonprofit educational purposes;

(2) The nature of the copyrighted work;

(3) The amount and substantiality of the portion used in relation to the copyrighted work as a whole; and

(4) The effect of the use upon the potential market for or value of the copyrighted work.

[Haworth co-indexing entry note]: "Appendix 1: Copyright Law." Croft, Janet Brennan. Co-published simultaneously in *Journal of Interlibrary Loan, Document Delivery & Information Supply* (The Haworth Information Press, an imprint of The Haworth Press, Inc.) Vol. 14, No. 3, 2004, pp. 47-69; and: *Legal Solutions in Electronic Reserves and the Electronic Delivery of Interlibrary Loan* (Janet Brennan Croft) The Haworth Information Press, an imprint of The Haworth Press, Inc., 2004, pp. 47-69. Single or multiple copies of this article are available for a fee from The Haworth Document Delivery Service [1-800-HAWORTH, 9:00 a.m. - 5:00 p.m. (EST). E-mail address: docdelivery@haworthpress.com].

http://www.haworthpress.com/web/JILIS
© 2004 by The Haworth Press, Inc. All rights reserved.
Digital Object Identifier: 10.1300/J110v14n03_07

The fact that a work is unpublished shall not itself bar a finding of fair use if such finding is made upon consideration of all the above factors.

§ 108. Limitations on Exclusive Rights: Reproduction by Libraries and Archives

(a) Except as otherwise provided in this title and notwithstanding the provisions of section 106, it is not an infringement of copyright for a library or archives, or any of its employees acting within the scope of their employment, to reproduce no more than one copy or phonorecord of a work, except as provided in subsections (b) and (c), or to distribute such copy or phonorecord, under the conditions specified by this section, if—

(1) The reproduction or distribution is made without any purpose of direct or indirect commercial advantage.

(2) The collections of the library or archives are (i) open to the public, or (ii) available not only to researchers affiliated with the library or archives or with the institution of which it is a part, but also to other persons doing research in a specialized field; and

(3) The reproduction or distribution of the work includes a notice of copyright that appears on the copy or phonorecord that is reproduced under the provisions of this section, or includes a legend stating that the work may be protected by copyright if no such notice can be found on the copy or phonorecord that is reproduced under the provisions of this section.

(b) The rights of reproduction and distribution under this section apply to three copies or phonorecords of an unpublished work duplicated solely for purposes of preservation and security or for deposit for research use in another library or archives of the type described by clause (2) of subsection (a), if—

(1) The copy or phonorecord reproduced is currently in the collections of the library or archives; and

(2) Any such copy or phonorecord that is reproduced in digital format is not otherwise distributed in that format and is not made available to the public in that format outside the premises of the library or archives.

(c) The right of reproduction under this section applies to three copies or phonorecords of a published work duplicated solely for the purpose of replacement of a copy or phonorecord that is damaged, deteriorating, lost, or stolen, or if the existing format in which the work is stored has become obsolete, if–

(1) The library or archives has, after a reasonable effort, determined that an unused replacement cannot be obtained at a fair price; and

(2) Any such copy or phonorecord that is reproduced in digital format is not made available to the public in that format outside the premises of the library or archives in lawful possession of such copy.

For purposes of this subsection, a format shall be considered obsolete if the machine or device necessary to render perceptible a work stored in that format is no longer manufactured or is no longer reasonably available in the commercial marketplace.

(d) The rights of reproduction and distribution under this section apply to a copy, made from the collection of a library or archives where the user makes his or her request or from that of another library or archives, of no more than one article or other contribution to a copyrighted collection or periodical issue, or to a copy or phonorecord of a small part of any other copyrighted work, if–

(1) The copy or phonorecord becomes the property of the user and the library or archives has had no notice that the copy or phonorecord would be used for any purpose other than private study, scholarship, or research; and

(2) The library or archives displays prominently, at the place where orders are accepted and includes on its order form, a warning of copyright in accordance with requirements that the Register of Copyrights shall prescribe by regulation.

(e) The rights of reproduction and distribution under this section apply to the entire work, or to a substantial part of it, made from the collection of a library or archives where the user makes his or her request or from that of another library or archives, if the library or archives has first determined, on the basis of a reasonable investigation, that a copy or phonorecord of the copyrighted work cannot be obtained at a fair price, if–

(1) The copy or phonorecord becomes the property of the user and the library or archives has had no notice that the copy or phonorecord

would be used for any purpose other than private study, scholarship, or research; and

(2) The library or archives displays prominently, at the place where orders are accepted and includes on its order form, a warning of copyright in accordance with requirements that the Register of Copyrights shall prescribe by regulation.

(f) Nothing in this section–

(1) Shall be construed to impose liability for copyright infringement upon a library or archives or its employees for the unsupervised use of reproducing equipment located on its premises: *Provided*, That such equipment displays a notice that the making of a copy may be subject to the copyright law;

(2) Excuses a person who uses such reproducing equipment or who requests a copy or phonorecord under subsection (d) from liability for copyright infringement for any such act, or for any later use of such copy or phonorecord, if it exceeds fair use as provided by section 107;

(3) Shall be construed to limit the reproduction and distribution by lending of a limited number of copies and excerpts by a library or archives of an audiovisual news program, subject to clauses (1), (2) and (3) of subsection (a); or

(4) In any way affects the right of fair use as provided by section 107, or any contractual obligations assumed at any time by the library or archives when it obtained a copy or phonorecord of a work in its collections.

(g) The rights of reproduction and distribution under this section extend to the isolated and unrelated reproduction or distribution of a single copy or phonorecord of the same material on separate occasions, but do not extend to cases where the library or archives, or its employee–

(1) Is aware or has substantial reason to believe that it is engaging in the related or concerted reproduction or distribution of multiple copies or phonorecords of the same material, whether made on one occasion or over a period of time and whether intended for aggregate use by one or more individuals or for separate use by the individual members of a group; or

(2) Engages in the systematic reproduction or distribution of single or multiple copies or phonorecords of material described in subsection (d): *Provided,* That nothing in this clause prevents a library or archives from participating in interlibrary arrangements that do not have, as their purpose or effect, that the library or archives receiving such copies or phonorecords for distribution does so in such aggregate quantities as to substitute for a subscription to or purchase of such work.

(h)(1) For purposes of this section, during the last 20 years of any term of copyright of a published work, a library or archives, including a nonprofit educational institution that functions as such, may reproduce, distribute, display, or perform in facsimile or digital form a copy or phonorecord of such work, or portions thereof, for purposes of preservation, scholarship, or research, if such library or archives has first determined, on the basis of a reasonable investigation, that none of the conditions set forth in subparagraphs (A), (B) and (C) of paragraph (2) apply.

(2) No reproduction, distribution, display, or performance is authorized under this subsection if–

(A) The work is subject to normal commercial exploitation.
(B) A copy or phonorecord of the work can be obtained at a reasonable price; or
(C) The copyright owner or its agent provides notice pursuant to regulations promulgated by the Register of Copyrights that either of the conditions set forth in subparagraphs (A) and (B) applies.

(3) The exemption provided in this subsection does not apply to any subsequent uses by users other than such library or archives.

(i) The rights of reproduction and distribution under this section do not apply to a musical work, a pictorial, graphic or sculptural work, or a motion picture or other audiovisual work other than an audiovisual work dealing with news, except that no such limitation shall apply with respect to rights granted by subsections (b) and (c), or with respect to pictorial or graphic works published as illustrations, diagrams, or similar adjuncts to works of which copies are reproduced or distributed in accordance with subsections (d) and (e).

§ 109. Limitations on Exclusive Rights: Effect of Transfer of Particular Copy or Phonorecord

(a) Notwithstanding the provisions of section 106(3), the owner of a particular copy or phonorecord lawfully made under this title, or any person authorized by such owner, is entitled, without the authority of the copyright owner, to sell or otherwise dispose of the possession of that copy or phonorecord. Notwithstanding the preceding sentence, copies or phonorecords of works subject to restored copyright under section 104A that are manufactured before the date of restoration of copyright or, with respect to reliance parties, before publication or service of notice under section 104A(e), may be sold or otherwise disposed of without the authorization of the owner of the restored copyright for purposes of direct or indirect commercial advantage only during the 12-month period beginning on–

(1) The date of the publication in the Federal Register of the notice of intent filed with the Copyright Office under section 104A(d)(2)(A), or

(2) The date of the receipt of actual notice served under section 104A(d) (2)(B), whichever occurs first.

(b)(1)(A) Notwithstanding the provisions of subsection (a), unless authorized by the owners of copyright in the sound recording or the owner of copyright in a computer program (including any tape, disk, or other medium embodying such program) and in the case of a sound recording in the musical works embodied therein, neither the owner of a particular phonorecord nor any person in possession of a particular copy of a computer program (including any tape, disk, or other medium embodying such program), may, for the purposes of direct or indirect commercial advantage, dispose of, or authorize the disposal of, the possession of that phonorecord or computer program (including any tape, disk, or other medium embodying such program) by rental, lease, or lending, or by any other act or practice in the nature of rental, lease, or lending. Nothing in the preceding sentence shall apply to the rental, lease, or lending of a phonorecord for nonprofit purposes by a nonprofit library or nonprofit educational institution. The transfer of possession of a lawfully made copy of a computer program by a nonprofit educational institution to another nonprofit educational institution or to faculty, staff and students does not constitute rental, lease, or lending for direct or indirect commercial purposes under this subsection.

(B) This subsection does not apply to–

(i) A computer program which is embodied in a machine or product and which cannot be copied during the ordinary operation or use of the machine or product; or
(ii) A computer program embodied in or used in conjunction with a limited purpose computer that is designed for playing video games and may be designed for other purposes.

(C) Nothing in this subsection affects any provision of chapter 9 of this title.

(2)(A) Nothing in this subsection shall apply to the lending of a computer program for nonprofit purposes by a nonprofit library, if each copy of a computer program, which is lent by such library, has affixed to the packaging containing the program a warning of copyright in accordance with requirements that the Register of Copyrights shall prescribe by regulation.

(B) Not later than three years after the date of the enactment of the Computer Software Rental Amendments Act of 1990 and at such times thereafter as the Register of Copyrights considers appropriate, the Register of Copyrights, after consultation with representatives of copyright owners and librarians, shall submit to the Congress a report stating whether this paragraph has achieved its intended purpose of maintaining the integrity of the copyright system while providing nonprofit libraries the capability to fulfill their function. Such report shall advise the Congress as to any information or recommendations that the Register of Copyrights considers necessary to carry out the purposes of this subsection.

(3) Nothing in this subsection shall affect any provision of the antitrust laws. For purposes of the preceding sentence, "antitrust laws" has the meaning given that term in the first section of the Clayton Act and includes section 5 of the Federal Trade Commission Act to the extent that section relates to unfair methods of competition.
(4) Any person who distributes a phonorecord or a copy of a computer program (including any tape, disk, or other medium embodying such program) in violation of paragraph (1) is an infringer of copyright under section 501 of this title and is subject to the remedies set forth in

sections 502, 503, 504, 505, and 509. Such violation shall not be a criminal offense under section 506 or cause such person to be subject to the criminal penalties set forth in section 2319 of title 18.

(c) Notwithstanding the provisions of section 106(5), the owner of a particular copy lawfully made under this title, or any person authorized by such owner, is entitled, without the authority of the copyright owner, to display that copy publicly, either directly or by the projection of no more than one image at a time, to viewers present at the place where the copy is located.

(d) The privileges prescribed by subsections (a) and (c) do not, unless authorized by the copyright owner, extend to any person who has acquired possession of the copy or phonorecord from the copyright owner, by rental, lease, loan, or otherwise, without acquiring ownership of it.

(e) Notwithstanding the provisions of sections 106(4) and 106(5), in the case of an electronic audiovisual game intended for use in coin-operated equipment, the owner of a particular copy of such a game lawfully made under this title, is entitled, without the authority of the copyright owner of the game, to publicly perform or display that game in coin-operated equipment, except that this subsection shall not apply to any work of authorship embodied in the audiovisual game if the copyright owner of the electronic audiovisual game is not also the copyright owner of the work of authorship.

§ 110. Limitations on Exclusive Rights: Exemption of Certain Performances and Displays

Notwithstanding the provisions of section 106, the following are not infringements of copyright:

(1) Performance or display of a work by instructors or pupils in the course of face-to-face teaching activities of a nonprofit educational institution, in a classroom or similar place devoted to instruction, unless, in the case of a motion picture or other audiovisual work, the performance, or the display of individual images, is given by means of a copy that was not lawfully made under this title and that the person responsible for the performance knew or had reason to believe was not lawfully made;

(2) Except with respect to a work produced or marketed primarily for performance or display as part of mediated instructional activities transmitted via digital networks, or a performance or display

that is given by means of a copy or phonorecord that is not lawfully made and acquired under this title and the transmitting government body or accredited nonprofit educational institution knew or had reason to believe was not lawfully made and acquired, the performance of a nondramatic literary or musical work or reasonable and limited portions of any other work, or display of a work in an amount comparable to that which is typically displayed in the course of a live classroom session, by or in the course of a transmission, if–

(A) The performance or display is made by, at the direction of, or under the actual supervision of an instructor as an integral part of a class session offered as a regular part of the systematic mediated instructional activities of a governmental body or an accredited nonprofit educational institution.

(B) The performance or display is directly related and of material assistance to the teaching content of the transmission;

(C) The transmission is made solely for, and, to the extent technologically feasible; the reception of such transmission is limited to–

(i) Students officially enrolled in the course for which the transmission is made; or

(ii) Officers or employees of governmental bodies as a part of their official duties or employment; and

(D) The transmitting body or institution–

(i) Institutes policies regarding copyright, provides informational materials to faculty, students and relevant staff members that accurately describe and promote compliance with, the laws of the United States relating to copyright and provides notice to students that materials used in connection with the course may be subject to copyright protection; and

(ii) In the case of digital transmissions–

(I) Applies technological measures that reasonably prevent–

(aa) Retention of the work in accessible form by recipients of the transmission from the transmitting body or institution for longer than the class session; and

(bb) unauthorized further dissemination of the work in accessible form by such recipients to others; and

(II)   Does not engage in conduct that could reasonably be expected to interfere with technological measures used by copyright owners to prevent such retention or unauthorized further dissemination;

(3) Performance of a nondramatic literary or musical work or of a dramatico-musical work of a religious nature, or display of a work, in the course of services at a place of worship or other religious assembly;

(4) Performance of a nondramatic literary or musical work otherwise than in a transmission to the public, without any purpose of direct or indirect commercial advantage and without payment of any fee or other compensation for the performance to any of its performers, promoters, or organizers, if–

(A) There is no direct or indirect admission charge; or

(B) The proceeds, after deducting the reasonable costs of producing the performance, are used exclusively for educational, religious, or charitable purposes and not for private financial gain, except where the copyright owner has served notice of objection to the performance under the following conditions:

(i)   The notice shall be in writing and signed by the copyright owner or such owner's duly authorized agent; and

(ii)   The notice shall be served on the person responsible for the performance at least seven days before the date of the performance and shall state the reasons for the objection; and

(iii)   The notice shall comply, in form, content and manner of service, with requirements that the Register of Copyrights shall prescribe by regulation;

(5)(A) except as provided in subparagraph (B), communication of a transmission embodying a performance or display of a work by the public reception of the transmission on a single receiving apparatus of a kind commonly used in private homes, unless–

(i) a direct charge is made to see or hear the transmission; or

(ii) the transmission thus received is further transmitted to the public;

[Portions Removed]

In paragraph (2), the term "mediated instructional activities" with respect to the performance or display of a work by digital transmission under this section refers to activities that use such work as an integral part of the class experience, controlled by or under the actual supervision of the instructor and analogous to the type of performance or display that would take place in a live classroom setting. The term does not refer to activities that use, in 1 or more class sessions of a single course, such works as textbooks, course packs, or other material in any media, copies or phonorecords of which are typically purchased or acquired by the students in higher education for their independent use and retention or are typically purchased or acquired for elementary and secondary students for their possession and independent use.

For purposes of paragraph (2), accreditation–

(A) with respect to an institution providing post-secondary education, shall be as determined by a regional or national accrediting agency recognized by the Council on Higher Education Accreditation or the United States Department of Education; and

(B) with respect to an institution providing elementary or secondary education, shall be as recognized by the applicable state certification or licensing procedures.

For purposes of paragraph (2), no governmental body or accredited nonprofit educational institution shall be liable for infringement by reason of the transient or temporary storage of material carried out through the automatic technical process of a digital transmission of the performance or display of that material as authorized under paragraph (2). No such material stored on the system or network controlled or operated by the transmitting body or institution under this paragraph shall be maintained on such system or network in a manner ordinarily accessible to anyone other than anticipated recipients. No such copy shall be maintained on the system or network in a manner ordinarily accessible to such anticipated recipients for a longer period than is reasonably necessary to facilitate the transmissions for which it was made.

AGREEMENT ON GUIDELINES FOR CLASSROOM COPYING IN NOT-FOR-PROFIT EDUCATIONAL INSTITUTIONS WITH RESPECT TO BOOKS AND PERIODICALS

The purpose of the following guidelines is to state the minimum and not the maximum standards of educational fair use under Section 107 of H.R. 2223 (this section). The parties agree that the conditions determining the extent of permissible copying for educational purposes may change in the future; that certain types of copying permitted under these guidelines may not be permissible in the future; and conversely that in the future other types of copying not permitted under these guidelines may be permissible under revised guidelines.

Moreover, the following statement of guidelines is not intended to limit the types of copying permitted under the standards of fair use under judicial decision and which are stated in Section 107 of the Copyright Revision Bill (this section). There may be instances in which copying which does not fall within the guidelines stated below may nonetheless be permitted under the criteria of fair use.

GUIDELINES

I. Single Copying for Teachers

A single copy may be made of any of the following by or for a teacher at his or her individual request for his or her scholarly research or use in teaching or preparation to teach a class:

    A. A chapter from a book;
    B. An article from a periodical or newspaper;
    C. A short story, short essay or short poem, whether or not from a collective work;
    D. A chart, graph, diagram, drawing, cartoon or picture from a book, periodical, or newspaper.

II. Multiple Copies for Classroom Use

Multiple copies (not to exceed in any event more than one copy per pupil in a course) may be made by or for the teacher giving the course for classroom use or discussion; provided that:

    A. The copying meets the tests of brevity and spontaneity as defined below; and,

B. Meets the cumulative effect test as defined below; and
C. Each copy includes a notice of copyright.

Definitions

Brevity

(i) Poetry:

(a) A complete poem if less than 250 words and if printed on not more than two pages or,
(b) from a longer poem, an excerpt of not more than 250 words.

(ii) Prose:

(a) Either a complete article, story or essay of less than 2,500 words, or
(b) an excerpt from any prose work of not more than 1,000 words or 10% of the work, whichever is less, but in any event a minimum of 500 words. (Each of the numerical limits stated in "i" and "ii" above may be expanded to permit the completion of an unfinished line of a poem or of an unfinished prose paragraph.)

(iii) Illustration: One chart, graph, diagram, drawing, cartoon or picture per book or per periodical issue.
(iv) "Special" works: Certain works in poetry, prose or in "poetic prose" which often combine language with illustrations and which are intended sometimes for children and at other times for a more general audience fall short of 2,500 words in their entirety. Paragraph "ii" above notwithstanding such "special works" may not be reproduced in their entirety; however, an excerpt comprising not more than two of the published pages of such special work and containing not more than 10% of the words found in the text thereof, may be reproduced.

Spontaneity

(i) The copying is at the instance and inspiration of the individual teacher and
(ii) The inspiration and decision to use the work and the moment of its use for maximum teaching effectiveness are so close in time that it would be unreasonable to expect a timely reply to a request for permission.

Cumulative Effect

(i)   The copying of the material is for only one course in the school in which the copies are made.

(ii)   Not more than one short poem, article, story, essay or two excerpts may be copied from the same author, nor more than three from the same collective work or periodical volume during one class term.

(iii)   There shall not be more than nine instances of such multiple copying for one course during one class term. (The limitations stated in "ii" and "iii" above shall not apply to current news periodicals, newspapers and current news sections of other periodicals.)

III. Prohibitions as to I and II Above

Notwithstanding any of the above, the following shall be prohibited:

(A)   Copying shall not be used to create or to replace or substitute for anthologies, compilations or collective works. Such replacement or substitution may occur whether copies of various works or excerpts therefrom are accumulated or reproduced and used separately.

(B)   There shall be no copying of or from works intended to be "consumable" in the course of study or of teaching. These include workbooks, exercises, standardized tests and test booklets and answer sheets and like consumable material.

(C)   Copying shall not:

(a)   substitute for the purchase of books, publishers' reprints or periodicals;

(b)   be directed by higher authority;

(c)   be repeated with respect to the same item by the same teacher from term to term.

(D)   No charge shall be made to the student beyond the actual cost of the photocopying.

Agreed March 19, 1976. Ad Hoc Committee on Copyright Law Revision: By Sheldon Elliott Steinbach.

CONTU GUIDELINES ON PHOTOCOPYING
UNDER INTERLIBRARY LOAN ARRANGEMENTS

Introduction

Subsection 108(g)(2) of the bill deals, among other things, with limits on interlibrary arrangements for photocopying. It prohibits systematic photocopying of copyrighted materials but permits interlibrary arrangements "that do not have, as their purpose or effect, that the library or archives receiving such copies or phonorecords for distribution does so in such aggregate quantities as to substitute for a subscription to or purchase of such work."

The National Commission on New Technological Uses of Copyrighted Works offered its good offices to the House and Senate subcommittees in bringing the interested parties together to see if agreement could be reached on what a realistic definition would be of "such aggregate quantities." The Commission consulted with the parties and suggested the interpretation that follows, on which there has been substantial agreement by the principal library, publisher and author organizations. The Commission considers the guidelines which follow to be a workable and fair interpretation of the intent of the proviso portion of subsection 108(g)(2).

These guidelines are intended to provide guidance in the application of section 108 to the most frequently encountered interlibrary case: a library's obtaining from another library, in lieu of interlibrary loan, copies of articles from relatively recent issues of periodicals–those published within five years prior to the date of the request. The guidelines do not specify what aggregate quantity of copies of an article or articles published in a periodical, the issue date of which is more than five years prior to the date when the request for the copy thereof is made, constitutes a substitute for a subscription to such periodical. The meaning of the proviso to subsection 108(g)(2) in such case is left to future interpretation.

The point has been made that the present practice on interlibrary loans and use of photocopies in lieu of loans may be supplemented or even largely replaced by a system in which one or more agencies or institutions, public or private, exist for the specific purpose of providing a central source for photocopies. Of course, these guidelines would not apply to such a situation.

Guidelines for the Proviso of Subsection 108(g)(2)

1. As used in the proviso of subsection 108(g)(2), the words ".... such aggregate quantities as to substitute for a subscription to or purchase of such work" shall mean:

(a) with respect to any given periodical (as opposed to any given issue of a periodical), filled requests of a library or archives (a "requesting entity") within any calendar year for a total of six or more copies of an article or articles published in such periodical within five years prior to the date of the request. These guidelines specifically shall not apply, directly or indirectly, to any request of a requesting entity for a copy or copies of an article or articles published in any issue of a periodical, the publication date of which is more than five years prior to the date when the request is made. These guidelines do not define the meaning, with respect to such a request, of ".... such aggregate quantities as to substitute for a subscription to [such periodical]."

(b) With respect to any other material described in subsection 108(d), including fiction and poetry, filled requests of a requesting entity within any calendar year for a total of six or more copies or phonorecords of or from any given work (including a collective work) during the entire period when such material shall be protected by copyright.

2. In the event that a requesting entity:

(a) shall have in force or shall have entered an order for a subscription to a periodical, or

(b) has within its collection, or shall have entered an order for, a copy of phonorecord of any other copyrighted work, materials from either category of which it desires to obtain by copy from another library or archives (the "supplying entity"), because the material to be copied is not reasonably available for use by the requesting entity itself, then the fulfillment of such request shall be treated as though the requesting entity made such copy from its own collection. A library or archives may request a copy or phonorecord from a supplying entity only under those circumstances where the requesting entity would have been able, under the other provisos of section 108, to supply such copy from materials in its own collection.

3. No request for a copy or phonorecord of any materials to which these guidelines apply may be fulfilled by the supplying entity unless such request is accompanied by a representation by the requesting entity that the request was made in conformity with these guidelines.

4. The requesting entity shall maintain records of all requests made by it for copies or phonorecords of any materials to which these guidelines apply and shall maintain records of the fulfillment of such requests, which records shall be retained until the end of the third complete calendar year after the end of the calendar year in which the respective request shall have been made.

5. As part of the review provided for in subsection 108(i), these guidelines shall be reviewed not later than five years from the effective date of this bill.

These guidelines were accepted by the Conference Committee and were incorporated into its report on the new act. During the ensuing twenty months, both library and publisher organizations have reported considerable progress toward adapting their practices to conform to the CONTU guidelines.

The guidelines specifically leave the status of periodical articles more than five years old to future determination. Moreover, institutions set up for the specific purpose of supplying photocopies of copyrighted material are excluded from coverage of the guidelines.

CONFU FAIR-USE GUIDELINES FOR ELECTRONIC RESERVE SYSTEMS (NOT APPROVED BY ALL PARTIES; FOR GUIDANCE ONLY)

Introduction

Many college, university and school libraries have established reserve operations for readings and other materials that support the instructional requirements of specific courses. Some educational institutions are now providing electronic reserve systems that allow storage of electronic versions of materials that students may retrieve on a computer screen and from which they may print a copy for their personal study. When materials are included as a matter of fair use, electronic reserve systems should constitute an ad hoc or supplemental source of information for students, beyond a textbook or other materials. If included with permission from the copyright owner, however, the scope and range of materials is potentially unlimited, depending upon the permission granted. Although fair use is determined on a case-by-case basis, the following guidelines identify an understanding of fair use for the reproduction, distribution, display and performance of materials in the context of creating and using an electronic reserve system.

Making materials accessible through electronic reserve systems raises significant copyright issues. Electronic reserve operations include the making of a digital version of text, the distribution and display of that version at workstations and downloading and printing of copies. The complexities of the electronic environment, and the growing potential for implicating copyright infringements, raise the need for a fresh understanding of fair use. These guidelines are not intended to burden the facilitation of reserves unduly, but instead offer a workable path that educators and librarians may follow in order to exercise a meaningful application of fair use, while also acknowledging and respecting the interests of copyright owners.

These guidelines focus generally on the traditional domain of reserve rooms, particularly copies of journal articles and book chapters and their accompanying graphics. Nevertheless, they are not meant to apply exclusively to textual materials and may be instructive for the fair use of other media. The guidelines also focus on the use of the complete article or the entire book chapter. Using only brief excerpts from such works would most likely also be fair use, possibly without all of the restrictions or conditions set forth in these guidelines. Operators of reserve systems should also provide safeguards for the integrity of the text and the author's reputation, including verification that the text is correctly scanned.

The guidelines address only those materials protected by copyright and for which the institution has not obtained permission before including them in an electronic reserve system. The limitations and conditions set forth in these guidelines need not apply to materials in the public domain–such as works of the U.S. government or works on which copyright has expired–or to works for which the institution has obtained permission for inclusion in the electronic reserve system. License agreements may govern the uses of some materials. Persons responsible for electronic reserve systems should refer to applicable license terms for guidance. If an instructor arranges for students to acquire a work by some means that includes permission from the copyright owner, the instructor should not include that same work on an electronic reserve system as a matter of fair use.

These guidelines are the outgrowth of negotiations among diverse parties attending the Conference on Fair Use ("CONFU") meetings sponsored by the Information Infrastructure Task Force's Working Group on Intellectual Property Rights. While endorsements of any guidelines by all conference participants are unlikely, these guidelines have been endorsed by the organizations whose names appear at the end. These guidelines are in furtherance of the Working Group's objective of encouraging negotiated guidelines of fair use.

This introduction is an integral part of these guidelines and should be included with the guidelines wherever they may be reprinted or adopted by a library, academic institution, or other organization or association. Any person or entity claims no copyright protection of these guidelines and anyone is free to reproduce and distribute this document without permission.

A. Scope of Material

1. In accordance with fair use (Section 107 of the U.S. Copyright Act), electronic reserve systems may include copyrighted materials at the request of a course instructor.

2. Electronic reserve systems may include short items (such as an article from a journal, a chapter from a book or conference proceedings, or a poem from a collected work) or excerpts from longer items. "Longer items" may include articles, chapters, poems and other works that are of such length as to constitute a substantial portion of a book, journal, or other work of which they may be a part. "Short items" may include articles, chapters, poems and other works of a customary length and structure as to be a small part of a book, journal, or other work, even if that work may be marketed individually.

3. Electronic reserve systems should not include any material unless the instructor, the library, or another unit of the educational institution possesses a lawfully obtained copy.

4. The total amount of material included in electronic reserve systems for a specific course as a matter of fair use should be a small proportion of the total assigned reading for a particular course.

B. Notices and Attributions

1. On a preliminary or introductory screen, electronic reserve systems should display a notice, consistent with the notice described in Section 108(f)(1) of the Copyright Act. The notice should include additional language cautioning against further electronic distribution of the digital work.

2. If a notice of copyright appears on the copy of a work that is included in an electronic reserve system, the following statement shall appear at some place where users will likely see it in connection with access to the particular work:

> "The work from which this copy is made includes this notice: [restate the elements of the statutory copyright notice: e.g., Copyright 1996, XXX Corp.]"

3. Materials included in electronic reserve systems should include appropriate citations or attributions to their sources.

C. Access and Use

1. Electronic reserve systems should be structured to limit access to students registered in the course for which the items have been placed on reserve and to instructors and staff responsible for the course or the electronic system.

2. The appropriate methods for limiting access will depend on available technology. Solely to suggest and not to prescribe options for implementation, possible methods for limiting access may include one or more of the following or other appropriate methods:

> (a) individual password controls or verification of a student's registration status; or
>
> (b) password system for each class; or
>
> (c) retrieval of works by course number or instructor name, but not by author or title of the work; or
>
> (d) access limited to workstations that are ordinarily used by, or are accessible to, only enrolled students or appropriate staff or faculty.

3. Students should not be charged specifically or directly for access to electronic reserve systems.

D. Storage and Reuse

1. Permission from the copyright holder is required if the item is to be reused in a subsequent academic term for the same course offered by the same instructor, or if the item is a standard assigned or optional reading for an individual course taught in multiple sections by many instructors.

2. Material may be retained in electronic form while permission is being sought or until the next academic term in which the material might be used, but in no event for more than three calendar years, including the year in which the materials are last used.

3. Short-term access to materials included on electronic reserve systems in previous academic terms may be provided to students who have not completed the course.

**AMERICAN LIBRARY ASSOCIATION MODEL POLICY
CONCERNING COLLEGE AND UNIVERSITY
PHOTOCOPYING FOR CLASSROOM, RESEARCH
AND LIBRARY RESERVE USE (SECTION ON RESERVES)**

Source: Model Policy Concerning College and University Photocopying for Classroom, Research and Library Reserve Use, American Library Association, Washington Office, Washington, DC, March 1982. ISBN: 0-9389-5624. ALA Publishing also sells this item for $1.50. Reprinted here by permission of the American Library Association.

C. Library Reserve Uses

At the request of a faculty member, a library may photocopy and place on reserve excerpts from copyrighted works in its collection in accordance with guidelines similar to those governing formal classroom distribution for face-to-face teaching discussed above. This University [College] believes that these guidelines apply to the library reserve shelf to the extent it functions as an extension of classroom readings or reflects an individual student's right to photocopy for his personal scholastic use under the doctrine of fair use. In general, librarians may photocopy materials for reserve room use for the convenience of students both in preparing class assignments and in pursuing informal educational activities which higher education requires, such as advanced independent study and research.

If the request calls for only one copy to be placed on reserve, the library may photocopy an entire article, or an entire chapter from a book, or an entire poem. Requests for multiple copies on reserve should meet the following guidelines:

1. the amount of material should be reasonable in relation to the total amount of material assigned for one term of a course taking into account the nature of the course, its subject matter and level, 17 U.S.C. SS107(1) and (3);

2. the number of copies should be reasonable in light of the number of students enrolled, the difficulty and timing of assignments and the number of other courses which may assign the same material, 17 U.S.C. SS107(1) and (3);

3. the material should contain a notice of copyright, see 17 U.S.C. SS401;

4. the effect of photocopying the material should not be detrimental to the market for the work. (In general, the library should own at least one copy of the work.) 17 U.S.C. SS107(4).

For example, a professor may place on reserve as a supplement to the course textbook a reasonable number of copies of articles from academic journals or chapters from trade books. A reasonable number of copies will in most instances be less than six, but factors such as the length or difficulty of the assignment, the number of enrolled students and the length of time allowed for completion of the assignment may permit more in unusual circumstances.

In addition, a faculty member may also request that multiple copies of photocopied, copyrighted material be placed on the reserve shelf if there is insufficient time to obtain permission from the copyright owner. For example, a professor may place on reserve several photocopies of an entire article from a recent issue of *Time* magazine or the *New York Times* in lieu of distributing a copy to each member of the class. If you are in doubt as to whether a particular instance of photocopying is fair use in the reserve reading room, you should waive any fee for such a use.

D. Uses of Photocopied Material Requiring Permission

1. repetitive copying: The classroom or reserve use of photocopied materials in multiple courses or successive years will normally require advance permission from the owner of the copyright, 17 U.S.C. SS107(3).

2. copying for profit: Faculty should not charge students more than the actual cost of photocopying the material, 17 U.S.C. SS107(1).

3. consumable works: The duplication of works that are consumed in the classroom, such as standardized tests, exercises and work-

books, normally requires permission from the copyright owner, 17 U.S.C. SS107(4).

4. creation of anthologies as basic text material for a course: Creation of a collective work or anthology by photocopying a number of copyrighted articles and excerpts to be purchased and used together as the basic text for a course will in most instances require the permission of the copyrighted owners. Such photocopying of a book and thus less likely to be deemed fair use, 17 U.S.C. SS107(4).

Appendix 2

Public Domain
and Free E-Material

THE PUBLIC DOMAIN

- When Works Pass Into the Public Domain:
  http://www.unc.edu/~unclng/public-d.htm

Laura Gasaway's detailed chart helps you navigate the muddy waters of copyright expiration. It has been updated to show the effects of the "Sonny Bono Act" on copyright terms.

SOURCES OF ELECTRONIC
OUT-OF-COPYRIGHT MATERIAL

There are many sources online for public-domain e-books and shorter works, both fiction and non-fiction. In some cases, a link to one of these resources could satisfy an electronic reserve or interlibrary loan request with no need to be concerned about fair use–providing a link to publicly available material is not a violation of copyright law. Many sites even have very obscure or foreign language resources. A caveat: Project Gutenberg of Australia is subject to a different schedule of copyright expiration. Items, which may be legal to display on their site, may not be

[Haworth co-indexing entry note]: "Appendix 2: Public Domain and Free E-Material." Croft, Janet Brennan. Co-published simultaneously in *Journal of Interlibrary Loan, Document Delivery & Information Supply* (The Haworth Information Press, an imprint of The Haworth Press, Inc.) Vol. 14, No. 3, 2004, pp. 71-73; and: *Legal Solutions in Electronic Reserves and the Electronic Delivery of Interlibrary Loan* (Janet Brennan Croft) The Haworth Information Press, an imprint of The Haworth Press, Inc., 2004, pp. 71-73. Single or multiple copies of this article are available for a fee from The Haworth Document Delivery Service [1-800-HAWORTH, 9:00 a.m. - 5:00 p.m. (EST). E-mail address: docdelivery@haworthpress.com].

http://www.haworthpress.com/web/JILIS
Digital Object Identifier: 10.1300/J110v14n03_08

legal to display on a U.S. site. The difficulty of disentangling jurisdiction may protect you (Rimmer 16), but the safest thing to do is run them through Gasaway's public domain chart before linking. As of February 2004, Australia's proposed Free Trade agreement with the U.S. included a clause to bring Australia's copyright term into compliance with ours. If this passes, Australia will have a similar 70-year copyright extension.

The Big Ones

Blackmask Online: *http://www.blackmask.com/page.php*
  A well-arranged site including nearly 13,000 titles; fiction, non-fiction, European languages, Oriental languages in translation, children's books.

The Online Book Page: *http://onlinebooks.library.upenn.edu/*
  University of Pennsylvania's listing of over 20,000 free books on the Web, English-language only.

Project Gutenberg: *http://promo.net/pg/*
  Over 6,000 free e-texts.

University of Virginia's EText Center: *http://etext.lib.virginia.edu/ebooks/*
  Over 1,800 books. Includes African-American, Native American and Civil War collections.

Bartleby.com: *http://www.bartleby.com/*
  Reference, verse, fiction, nonfiction.

Australian

eBooks@Adelaide: *http://etext.library.adelaide.edu.au/*
  The University of Adelaide's collection of over 500 texts.

Project Gutenberg Australia: *http://promo.net/pg/pgau.html*
  Note their disclaimer: works by authors who died before 1951 are in the public domain in Australia, but not in the United States or many other countries.

Small or Specialized

The Latin Library: *http://www.thelatinlibrary.com/*
  Books in Latin

Christian Classics Ethereal Library: *http://www.ccel.org/*
   Multi-denominational; fiction, nonfiction, apologetics, translations.

An Online Library of Literature: *http://www.literature.org*
   A small selection of classic authors.

Perseus Digital Library: *http://www.perseus.tufts.edu/*
   Primarily classical and English renaissance texts, but also some American and other history.

International Children's Digital Library: *http://www.icdlbooks.org/*

Alex Catalog of Electronic Texts: *http://www.infomotions.com/alex/*
   English and American literature, philosophy.

Victorian Women Writers Project: *http://www.indiana.edu/~letrs/vwwp/*

Academy of American Poets: *http://www.poets.org/index.cfm*

American Verse Project: *http://www.hti.umich.edu/a/amverse/*

19th Century Women's Poetry:
http://www.unl.edu/legacy/19cwww/books/elibe/poetry.htm#list

Appendix 3

Tools

SOURCES OF PERMISSIONS

Copyright Clearance Center, Inc.: *http://www.copyright.com/*
The major source for permissions for print materials.

Copyright Office Records: *http://www.copyright.gov/records/*
Search records back to 1978 for copyrighted material in a number of categories. Also see *http://www.copyright.gov/circs/circ22.html* for instructions on how to search a copyright.

Music Publisher's Association:
http://www.mpa.org/copyright/searchenter.html
This site can help you find the publisher for a piece of music; it searches the archives of the three major music rights suppliers (ASCAP, BMI and SESAC) at once.

Getting Permission:
http://www.utsystem.edu/ogc/intellectualproperty/permissn.htm
The ever-helpful UT site on copyright includes an extensive list of permission sources, including sources for materials other than print and music. Try this if it isn't available through the sources listed above.

[Haworth co-indexing entry note]: "Appendix 3: Tools." Croft, Janet Brennan. Co-published simultaneously in *Journal of Interlibrary Loan, Document Delivery & Information Supply* (The Haworth Information Press, an imprint of The Haworth Press, Inc.) Vol. 14, No. 3, 2004, pp. 75-78; and: *Legal Solutions in Electronic Reserves and the Electronic Delivery of Interlibrary Loan* (Janet Brennan Croft) The Haworth Information Press, an imprint of The Haworth Press, Inc., 2004, pp. 75-78. Single or multiple copies of this article are available for a fee from The Haworth Document Delivery Service [1-800-HAWORTH, 9:00 a.m. - 5:00 p.m. (EST). E-mail address: docdelivery@haworthpress.com].

COPYRIGHT RESOURCES ON THE WEB

United States Copyright Office: *http://www.loc.gov/copyright/*
An excellent source of authoritative information all in one place. Includes text of all relevant laws, information about pending legislation, how to register items for copyright and much more.

Legal Information Institute: *http://www4.law.cornell.edu/uscode/17/*
Includes not just the text of the U.S. Code on Copyrights, but also notes, updates and other references.

Copyright Quickguide: *http://www.copyright.iupui.edu/quickguide.htm*
Indiana University/Purdue University at Indianapolis; Kenneth Crews' guide to copyright for educators.

Coalition for Networked Information: *http://www.cni.org*
Especially useful is a collection of American Library Association policies at *http://www.cni.org/docs/infopols/ALA.html*, including copyright, ILL, confidentiality and freedom to read.

Stanford University Libraries Copyright and Fair Use page:
http://fairuse.stanford.edu/index.html
A wealth of useful information, including a list of copyright cases relevant to libraries.

Copyright Crash Course:
http://www.utsystem.edu/OGC/IntellectualProperty/cprtindx.htm
Georgia Harper's University of Texas page.

Library Law: *http://www.librarylaw.com/index.html*
Mary Minow's wide-ranging site on all aspects of library law.

RESERVES RESOURCES

Electronic Reserves Clearinghouse:
http://www.mville.edu/administration/Staff/Jeff_Rosedale/
An extensive and up-to-date list of links on many aspects of electronic reserves. Includes links to sample policies.

Copyright and Electronic Reserves:
http://www.utsystem.edu/ogc/intellectualproperty/ereserve.htm
Georgia Harper's overview of copyright and electronic reserves is an excellent resource for librarians and faculty alike.

ReserveWeb Links: *http://reserveweb.bard.edu/links.htm*
A nice list of links from Bard College.

Music Library Association Guidelines:
http://www.lib.jmu.edu/org/mla/Guidelines/
Includes guidelines for both electronic and physical reserves for music.

INTERLIBRARY LOAN RESOURCES

ILLWeb Codes and Guidelines: *http://www.illweb.org/codes.htm*
Links to all the relevant guidelines in one place.

IFLANET Interlibrary loan links: *http://www.ifla.org/II/ill.htm*

Copyright in the Library: Interlibrary Loan:
http://www.utsystem.edu/ogc/intellectualproperty/l-108g.htm
Georgia Harper's UT site.

www.Lesmorris.com
Home pages for the *Journal of Interlibrary Loan, Document Delivery & Information Supply* (with a special emphasis on Electronic Reserve) and The Interlibrary Loan Policies Directory, 7th ed., 2002

LIST-SERVS AND DISCUSSION GROUPS

Liblicense: *http://www.library.yale.edu/~llicense/*
Licensing issues, including negotiating contracts.

Association of Research Libraries Electronic Reserves Discussion List:
arl-ereserve@arl.org
Send an e-mail with SUBSCRIBE in the subject line.

Docutek E-Res Users Group: *ereserves@docutek.com*
A good source of information on e-reserves, even if you do not use
E-Res. Send an email with SUBSCRIBE in the subject line.

CNI Copyright Forum: *http://www.cni.org/Hforums/cni-copyright/*
Specifically devoted to copyright issues.

ILL-L: *listproc@northwestern.edu*

A very active international interlibrary loan discussion list. Send message saying "subscribe ILL-L firstname lastname."

ARIE-L: *listserv@listserv.idbsu.edu*

For discussion of the ARIEL interlibrary loan electronic document delivery system.

Bibliography

CASES CITED

American Geophysical Union v. Texaco, Inc., 60 F. 3rd 913, 923 (2nd Cir. 1994), cert. dismissed, 616 U.S. 1005 (1995).

Basic Books v. Kinko's, 758 F. Supp. 1522 (S.D.N.Y. 1991).

Hotaling v. Church of Jesus Christ of Latter-Day Saints, 118 F. 3rd 199 (4th Cir. 1997).

Princeton University Press v. Michigan Documents Service, 99 F. 3d 1381 (6th Cir. 1996), cert. denied, 520 U.S. 1156 (1997).

Religious Technology Center v. NETCOM, 907 F. Supp. 1361 (N.D. Cal. 1995).

Ryan v. Carl Corporation, 23 F. Supp. 2d 1146 (N.D. Cal. 1998).

Tasini v. The New York Times Co., 192 F. 3d 356 (2nd Cir. 1999) amended 206 F.3rd 161, affirmed 533 U.S. 483 (2001).

Williams & Wilkins v. National Library of Medicine, 487 F. 2d. 1345 (Ct. Cl. 1973), affirmed 420 U.S. 376 (1975).

WORKS CITED

Brennan, Patricia, Karen Hersey and Georgia Harper. *Licensing Electronic Resources: Strategic and Practical Considerations for Licensing Electronic Information Delivery Agreements.* 23 July 2002. Association of Research Libraries. Available: http://arl.cni.org/scomm/licensing/licbooklet.html. 15 September 2003.

[Haworth co-indexing entry note]: "Bibliography." Croft, Janet Brennan. Co-published simultaneously in *Journal of Interlibrary Loan, Document Delivery & Information Supply* (The Haworth Information Press, an imprint of The Haworth Press, Inc.) Vol. 14, No. 3, 2004, pp. 79-81; and: *Legal Solutions in Electronic Reserves and the Electronic Delivery of Interlibrary Loan* (Janet Brennan Croft) The Haworth Information Press, an imprint of The Haworth Press, Inc., 2004, pp. 79-81. Single or multiple copies of this article are available for a fee from The Haworth Document Delivery Service [1-800-HAWORTH, 9:00 a.m. - 5:00 p.m. (EST). E-mail address: docdelivery@haworthpress.com].

http://www.haworthpress.com/web/JILIS
© 2004 by The Haworth Press, Inc. All rights reserved.
Digital Object Identifier: 10.1300/J110v14n03_10

Circular 21: Reproduction of Copyrighted Works by Educators and Librarians. June 1998. United States Copyright Office. Available: http://www.copyright.gov/circs/circ21.pdf. 3 September 2003.

CONTU Guidelines on Photocopying under Interlibrary Loan Arrangements. *3* July 2002 2003. Coalition for Networked Information. Available: http://www.cni.org/docs/infopols/CONTU.html. 29 August 2003.

Copyright Basics. 28 April 2003. United States Copyright Office. Available: http://www.copyright.gov/circs/circ1.html#wwp. 26 August 2003.

Copyright Law of the United States. June 2003. United States Copyright Office. Available: http://www.copyright.gov/title17/. 27 August 2003.

Crews, Kenneth D. *Copyright Essentials for Librarians and Educators*. Chicago: American Library Association, 2000.

Croft, Janet Brennan. "Model Licenses and Interlibrary Loan/Document Delivery from Electronic Resources." *Interlending and Document Supply* 29.4 (2001): 165-68.

Croft, Janet Brennan and Molly Murphy. "Licensing and the Interlibrary Loan Workflow." *Journal of Access Services* 1.2 (2002): 5-14.

Fair-Use Guidelines for Electronic Reserve Systems. 12 November 2001 1996. University of Texas. Available: http://www.utsystem.edu/ogc/intellectualproperty/rsrvguid.htm. 16 September 2003.

Gasaway, Laura N. "Copyright Considerations for Electronic Reserves." *Managing Electronic Reserves*. Ed. Jeff Rosedale. Chicago: American Library Association, 2002. 109-35.

_____. *Copyright Law in the Digital Age: Course Materials*. Chapel Hill NC: Laura N. Gasaway, 2000.

Gilmer, Lois C. *Interlibrary Loan: Theory and Management*. Englewood CO: Libraries Unlimited, 1994.

Harper, Georgia. *Acquisition under Contract*. 6 February 2003. University of Texas. Available: http://www.utsystem.edu/ogc/intellectualproperty/l-cntrct.htm. 29 August 2003.

_____. *CONFU Background*. 11 June 1997. University of Texas Copyright Crash Course. Available: http://www.utsystem.edu/ogc/intellectualproperty/confu2.htm. 3 September 2003.

_____. *Fair Use of Copyrighted Materials*. 14 November 2002. University of Texas. Available: http://www.utsystem.edu/ogc/intellectualproperty/copypol2.htm. 15 September 2003.

_____. *Fair Use: Reserve Room Operations, Generally*. 30 January 2003. University of Texas. Available: http://www.utsystem.edu/ogc/intellectualproperty/l-resgen.htm. 3 September 2003.

Heins, Marjorie. *"The Progress of Science and the Useful Arts": Why Copyright Today Threatens Intellectual Freedom.* Fall 2003. The Free Expression Policy Project. Available: http://www.fepproject. org/policyreports/copyright2dexsum.html. 17 September 2003.

In Wake of Declassified Report, ALA Renews Call for Legislative Amendments to Patriot Act. 2003. American Library Association. Available: http://www.ala.org//Content/ContentGroups/Press_Releases2/Press_ Releases_2003_September/ALA_renews_call_for_legislative_amendments_ to_Patriot_Act.htm. 19 September 2003.

Jackson, Mary E. "Perspective of the Association of Research Libraries." *Managing Electronic Reserves.* Ed. Jeff Rosedale. Chicago: American Library Association, 2002. 168-80.

Krause, Jason. "See Ya, UCITA." *American Bar Association Journal (ABA Journal)* (2003): 20.

Minow, Mary. *How I Learned to Love Fair Use . . .* 2003. Stanford University Libraries Copyright and Fair Use. Available: http://fairuse.stanford. edu/commentary_and_analysis/2003_07_minow.html. 30 July 2003.

Rimmer, Matthew. *The Dead Poets Society: The Copyright Term and the Public Domain.* 2003. First Monday. Available: http://www.firstmonday. dk/issues/issue8_6/rimmer/. 17 June 2003.

Rosedale, Jeff. "Conclusion." *Managing Electronic Reserves.* Ed. Jeff Rosedale. Chicago: American Library Association, 2002. 181-82.

Webster, Duane. *The Practical Realities of the New Copyright Laws: A Librarian's Perspective.* 2002. Association of Research Libraries. Available: http://www.arl.org/info/frn/copy/WebsterMLA02.html. 11 February 2003.

Index

Numbers followed by "n" indicate note.

BOOK ORDER FORM!

Order a copy of this book with this form or online at:
http://www.haworthpress.com/store/product.asp?sku=5250

Legal Solutions in Electronic Reserves
and the Electronic Delivery of Interlibrary Loan

_____ in softbound at $19.95 (ISBN: 0-7890-2559-0)
_____ in hardbound at $29.95 (ISBN: 0-7890-2558-2)

COST OF BOOKS _____

POSTAGE & HANDLING _____
US: $4.00 for first book & $1.50
for each additional book
Outside US: $5.00 for first book
& $2.00 for each additional book.

SUBTOTAL _____

In Canada: add 7% GST. _____

STATE TAX _____
CA, IL, IN, MN, NY, OH & SD residents
please add appropriate local sales tax.

FINAL TOTAL _____
If paying in Canadian funds, convert
using the current exchange rate,
UNESCO coupons welcome.

❑BILL ME LATER:
Bill-me option is good on US/Canada/
Mexico orders only; not good to jobbers,
wholesalers, or subscription agencies.

❑ Signature _____

❑ Payment Enclosed: $ _____

❑ PLEASE CHARGE TO MY CREDIT CARD:

❑ Visa ❑ MasterCard ❑ AmEx ❑ Discover
❑ Diner's Club ❑ Eurocard ❑ JCB

Account # _____

Exp Date _____

Signature _____
(Prices in US dollars and subject to change without notice.)

PLEASE PRINT ALL INFORMATION OR ATTACH YOUR BUSINESS CARD

Name

Address

City   State/Province   Zip/Postal Code

Country

Tel   Fax

E-Mail

May we use your e-mail address for confirmations and other types of information? ❑Yes ❑No We appreciate receiving
your e-mail address. Haworth would like to e-mail special discount offers to you, as a preferred customer.
We will never share, rent, or exchange your e-mail address. We regard such actions as an invasion of your privacy.

Order From Your **Local Bookstore** or Directly From
The Haworth Press, Inc. 10 Alice Street, Binghamton, New York 13904-1580 • USA
Call Our toll-free number (1-800-429-6784) / Outside US/Canada: (607) 722-5857
Fax: 1-800-895-0582 / Outside US/Canada: (607) 771-0012
E-mail your order to us: orders@haworthpress.com

For orders outside US and Canada, you may wish to order through your local
sales representative, distributor, or bookseller.
For information, see http://haworthpress.com/distributors

(Discounts are available for individual orders in US and Canada only, not booksellers/distributors.)

Please photocopy this form for your personal use.
www.HaworthPress.com

BOF04